taking tea in the medina

PENGUIN BOOKS

taking tea in the medina

Julie Le Clerc

Photography John Bougen & Julie Le Clerc

CONTENTS

INTRODUCTION

Rose water-drenched pastries and fragments of *halva* sit beside ornate tea glasses that tinkle on a beaten metal tray as they are swept through the dusty *medina* to our waiting thirst. We sip the sweet, fragrant tea, simultaneously tasting refreshment and the generous warmth of hospitality. The floral confections and sesame sweetmeats provide a different welcome — a taste of something truly magical.

The pursuit of novel tastes has inspired travellers for centuries. This is the story of one such culinary journey – it tells of my quest to discover authentic recipes and the background to these recipes. It reflects my constant search for flavour and integrity in food.

This tale is about deliciously honest recipes, of course, but it also contains many methods, secrets and stories of people who cook and live in the fascinating culinary landscape of the Middle East. Through the pages of this book, it is my pleasure to share with you time-honoured recipes from real cooks, interwoven with travel stories and recollections expressed through food.

For me, this book began a long time ago, as notions of the Middle East have enchanted me since I was a small child when I listened to stories my mother told of her kind and generous Lebanese granddad, Samuel Saleem Bishara, and I dreamed of his mysterious homeland. My curiosity began to expand when

I discovered my great-grandfather's treasured Bible written in Arabic script. I also cherished a real scarab beetle and some achingly fragile Egyptian lace that belonged to my paternal grandmother, gifts sent to her from a friend based in Egypt during the First World War. As a young girl, I was strangely attracted to images of pyramids and I quietly accumulated a private collection of these mystical icons.

Growing up to become a professional cook, food writer and culinary traveller allowed me to feed my long-time interest in the extraordinary food and culinary traditions of Middle Eastern countries. This book, therefore, is as much about my own culinary voyage as it is about what I found along the way.

When I first travelled in my youth, I spent several months camping (I kid you not) and journeying overland through Turkey, Iran, Syria, Jordan, Israel, and Egypt, then by ferry across the Mediterranean Sea to Greece. I was deeply impressed by many tastes I had not experienced before:

08

pillows of pita bread hot from the oven; *shawarma*, *okra*, halva; syrup-drenched pastries, and so on. I was captivated by the vivid flavours, freshness and vitality of the dishes and haunted by this cuisine's ability to resonate with the past. I can close my eyes, still, and experience again the distinct aroma, tastes and textures that these exotic foods held, just as if it were yesterday.

At this time, I longed most especially to visit Lebanon. Unfortunately, my first Middle Eastern journey was during the time of Lebanon's devastating civil war and I did not have the courage to enter the country. Years later, a chance meeting with devoted Middle Eastern traveller John Bougen led us to plan an extended joint adventure. Joyfully, our first stop was Lebanon, and so my dream to explore this country came true.

Lebanon is a delight. And while I found it meaningful to see the markings of history on this landscape of beauty, it is the overwhelming good nature of the Lebanese people and their ability to show this generosity through food that will remain deeply etched in my heart. Sadly, despite many efforts, I was unable to find any familial links during this visit. However, discovering Lebanon remains a particular pleasure for me. I feel that Lebanon is my culinary homeland, and somewhere I hope to return to again and again.

Onwards we roamed, from Azerbaijan to Egypt; from Turkey to the Gulf States; we cruised up the Nile and down the Bosphorus, eating with relish every step of the way. And all the while we learned lessons about culture and tradition, and about cooking and eating, through sharing food and drink with strangers. With only a smattering of Arabic between us, it was most certainly the language of food that brought us together with the good people we met along the way.

We were gifted time and again with the extraordinary experience of sharing authentic foods in the lands of their origin. From cooking in a homely kitchen in Baku with our Azerbaijani friends, to discussing ancient Arabic food history with a veiled woman in Dubai; we were honoured as guests and presented with food and recipes. From being invited by a stranger in a *souk* in Tripoli (Lebanon) to share a modest family meal, to savouring a lavish feast while cruising the Nile; all the dishes we experienced were enlightening.

Everywhere we went we were treated with unrestrained warmth, generosity and kindness. And while these experiences may sound remarkable, in reality, they're common occurrences – delightful encounters that confirm the renowned hospitality of Middle Eastern people.

Often blanketed as one cuisine, the subject of 'Middle Eastern food' is vast – to simplify it with a single name can deprecate its diversity and range. While there are many connecting culinary characteristics between countries, there are as many similarities as there are differences. Even compiling a list of countries that we in the West generally think of as 'Middle Eastern' can vary. Due to the historical movements of people and borders, political and even geographical listings are complicated. And interestingly, the people of the Middle East will consider themselves Oriental – a term Westerners are more likely to use to indicate the Far East.

The history of these regions is long and convoluted – far too elaborate to document here. However, it can be said that the food culture of today reflects this colourful history. The ancient Romans and Greeks, Persians, Arabs, Turks, Kurds, Ottomans and others have all left culinary legacies, ingredients and persuasions throughout this region. As a result, many dishes from different countries in the Middle East can be thought of as closely related.

The final cluster of Middle Eastern countries covered here is therefore a personal one. While there's an obvious base group, I have included certain countries because I feel their

cooking is strongly connected. For example, I have chosen to include Azerbaijan in this book because this now Baltic State was historically part of Northern Ancient Persia. Furthermore, due to the various culinary traditions introduced by former Ottoman rulers, Azerbaijani cuisine today bares many similarities to Turkish food.

While some Middle Eastern cook books may include Morocco, Tunisia and Algeria because of their culinary similarities – I have omitted these North African countries from my list, because of their distinct culinary differences. In fact, because Moroccan food and travel is so distinctive, we devoted our previous book, *Made in Morocco*, to that country alone.

From savouring traditional dishes in their countries of origin, I have observed many unifying ingredients and inclinations. I found that fresh, clean, uncomplicated flavours predominate. Generous use is made of tart flavours cast from ingredients such as lemons, pomegranates, *sumac* and yoghurt – ingredients that give many dishes a characteristic sour taste. The dominant herbs (parsley, mint and coriander) that grow in the region star as main players in often simple but always uniquely flavoursome dishes.

As a result of its position on the spice trade routes between the East and the West, many traditional dishes incorporate a dizzying combination of exotic spices. This is alluringly aromatic food, which often combines sweet-and-sour flavours and the sunburnt taste of exotic spices. Yet, while certain dishes may be pleasantly spicy, they are not necessarily hot.

I have grouped the dishes by type rather than origin because it is the ingredients themselves that are the most important keys to recreating this distinctly different cuisine. While some ingredients are ordinary, and therefore pleasing in their familiarity, others seem to hold almost magical qualities.

Consider mysterious sumac, a deep crimson powder ground from a berry that emulates the sourness of lemons; and earthy-flavoured saffron, a spice worth more than its weight in gold. Ancient pomegranates, exploding with lustrous, ruby-red seeds and bittersweet juice, and elaborately perfumed flower waters, distilled from roses or orange blossoms, are equally bewitching.

Once these exotic ingredients would have been hard to find. Now, they are globally available in supermarkets and delicatessens. The only ingredients I've found hard to purchase outside their country of origin are *frankincense* and *mastic*, both of which impart a particular fragrance to foods, and while interesting to experience, neither are essential to any particular recipe here.

To tie together the unifying threads of this vast topic, I have woven classic ingredients into chapters based around themes common to all the Middle Eastern countries we visited. With each chapter, I introduce and explain distinctive ingredients and share some typical recipes. While some ingredients overlap different categories, I have aimed to place each in the chapter where they are most clearly aligned with the chapter theme.

Naturally, any definitive list of Middle Eastern recipes would be immense and I have fretted over my desire to pay tribute to this remarkable cuisine in one single book. The recipes here simply illustrate my travel and taste memories. While the recipes I have chosen represent only a modest selection from all the many possibilities, they are limited by the pages of this book and not by a lack of choice.

Within my selection of recipes you will find some obvious but crucial choices, such as *hummus, falafel* and *baklava* – here I give you my own versions of these staples that I make at home. I have also included some personal favourites, like *fattoush*, date-filled *ma'amoul* and rose petal jam. I naturally hope that you will discover some unexpected finds here too, such

12

as pickled grapes, lamb and rhubarb stew, carrot jam, and Middle Eastern *mousakha'a*, to name but a few.

I found that several countries would claim to be the birthplace of one particular recipe or another. Even extensive research may only serve to uphold these conflicting claims. And every cook I met throughout the region believed wholeheartedly that his or her version of a particular recipe was the best version. Such is the pride of the cooks of the Middle East.

Many of the recipes in this book have come from these traditional cooks and, with their permission, it is my delight to pass on their valuable culinary knowledge. Cooking in these lands follows an oral tradition – recipes are handed down through generations, from mother to daughter, and so on. Dishes are made to taste without perfect measurements or specific directions. Instructions calling for an intuitive pinch of this or a practised handful of that meant that writing down precise measurements was also not an exact process. However, through extensive testing, I have endeavoured to develop these recipes to suit modern Western kitchens and practices.

The dishes that appear from Middle Eastern kitchens display many remarkable qualities. This is a varied, tasty and healthy cuisine, infused with an 'otherworldly' dimension. Layered with vivid flavours, which echo a colourful past imbued with history and tradition, this food possesses a definite sense of place. It is not overly refined or extravagant in its presentation – the beauty of this food lies in its authenticity.

This book, therefore, is not about reworking traditional recipes for the sake of change – it is about presenting time-honoured recipes to you. Where I may have tweaked the odd detail, this is only for the sake of ease of preparation and to

aid busy modern-world cooks. For instance, historically, cooking in these lands was manually laborious and indeed remains this way in many villages. Today, an electric food processor can be used to achieve many of these once time-consuming jobs, such as puréeing hummus or mincing meat. While I do take advantage of such modern methods, my aim has always been to do so with respect for the integrity of the ingredients and the cultural heritage of the recipes.

Today, Middle Eastern cuisine is enjoying huge popularity around the world, not only because of its vibrancy and healthfulness, but also because of its exoticism. It is these characteristics that gift Middle Eastern dishes with the ability to transport diners on an enchanted voyage through the sensation of taste.

A particular pleasure of researching this book came from my love of photography. With our travel shots, John and I concentrated on the culinary landscape – vibrant markets, raw ingredients, spice stores, cooks working in their kitchens, as well as authentic locations and scenery. And for me, being able to capture food on film completes the creative process of cooking and presenting food attractively that I relish.

I travel primarily for food experiences, which naturally involve and reflect people and cultures. As I gather recipes along the way, I find these culinary souvenirs serve as taste memories – provocative triggers that remind me of the people I have met and of places I have been, as much as meals I have eaten. In my experience, sharing food brings not only the joy of human kindness, but it gives meaning to the food.

Returning to the Middle East has increased my knowledge of and affection for the fascinating cuisine of these lands. If you choose to join me on my culinary journey and follow the food traditions of these exotic places, I know you will be richly rewarded with freshness, vibrancy and warm spirits. *JLee*

the mezze table
small appetising tastes

I gaze in delight at the *mezze* table laden with an astonishing array of dishes. Today, we are enjoying the riches of the kitchen at the Grand Hyatt Hotel in Amman, Jordan. In the mezze tradition, this series of vivid tastes is being served as an appetiser or first course.

Beside a neat stack of flatbread – an important mezze element always present – are bowls lavishly filled with different creamy dips. There's eggplant *moutabal* (*baba ghanoush*); *tagan* (sesame *taratour*); red pepper *muhammara*, and chickpea hummus. These purées are adorned in different ways too, from a dusting of paprika to a drizzle of green olive oil or a scattering of jewel-like pomegranate seeds.

Cradled on drifts of ice are large bowls of classic Middle Eastern salads – there's *tabbouleh*; Oriental salad; carrot with mint; potato and dill; and my favourite fattoush. This fattoush has been made with a clever twist and is a great example of how, within the bounds of custom, cooks will often modify traditional dishes to personalise a recipe. Here, in place of the usual small fragments of crisp bread that are tossed with the salad ingredients, this salad is cleverly topped with decorative long shards of fried pita bread.

I am drawn to the wonderful selection of savoury pastries. There are flaky pastry crescents packed with lamb; sour spinach and pine nut-stuffed triangles; and rolled cigar shapes filled with salty cheese and mint. With each mouthful, the warm pastries dissolve in my mouth to expose these flavoursome fillings.

While hotels and restaurants throughout the Middle East skilfully turn out very elaborate displays of mezze, in domestic situations grand displays are generally reserved for formal celebrations. At home, mezze may be a modest few dishes, such as a bowl of briny olives, a bunch of mint, and a thick slice of white cheese; or traditional salads served at room temperature.

During our travels, we enjoy many different forms of mezze, from basic to grand selections. We find one delightfully uncomplicated mezze experience at the quaint Istambouli Restaurant in Hamra, Beirut. Stepping down into this subterranean space is like stepping back in time to another charming era. Here we are presented for the first of many times

with an arrangement that initially appears to be a centrepiece or table adornment. This consists of whole sweet peppers that can be eaten like apples; lengths of Lebanese cucumber (the smaller, sweeter ones); crisp hearts of Romaine lettuce; and bouquets of fresh mint, flat-leaf parsley and radish. We soon realise that this is a complimentary mezze plate. We find these raw, crunchy, fresh vegetables, eaten as a separate course, a very refreshing way to start our meal.

Another memorable meal is our evening spent with Houda Bouri, aunt of my friend Greg Malouf, whom we have the pleasure of visiting at her home in Beirut. This evening Houda takes us to her favourite seafood restaurant, Sultan Brahim, situated on the main highway leading out of Beirut. Here, Houda guides us through an extraordinary meal with great charm and humour.

We begin with mezze. Houda shows us how to eat 'caviar' – a strange name for a dish that is actually shavings of dried fish garnished with garlic and olive oil. With one hand, Houda deftly gathers up a morsel of fish in a fragment of pita bread, at the same time mopping up the olive oil, then she elegantly manoeuvres this combination into her mouth. We attempt to do the same. It seems proficiency, but not grace, does come with practice.

Other notable mezze dishes from this feast include chickpeas cooked until softly melting into extra virgin olive oil and perfumed with cumin; classic eggplant purée adorned with pomegranate seeds; and crisply blanched almonds sitting in a bowl of ice cubes.

Mezze is an interactive, communal style of eating that spills over to the main course, when food is also brought to the centre of the table and shared. And between courses, we are offered the luxury of hot towels sensually drenched in orange flower water to cleanse our hands.

SMOKY EGGPLANT PURÉE baba ganoush / moutabal

Baba ghanoush means 'father of greediness' in English, and as this creamy dip is highly addictive I can well understand the translation. This smoky eggplant purée is also known as moutabal in some Middle Eastern countries, such as Lebanon, where it is usually made with the addition of tahini. I prefer to follow the Turkish tradition of substituting yoghurt for the tahini, as this gives a lighter yet creamier result to the baba ghanoush.

1kg (2 large) eggplants
2 tablespoons tahini or *labneh* (see page 120), or substitute thick yoghurt
2 cloves garlic, crushed
juice of 2–3 lemons, to taste
sea salt & freshly ground black pepper

garnish options
extra virgin olive oil
sprinkling of ground paprika
some fresh pomegranate seeds
chopped fresh parsley or mint leaves

makes 1½ cups

1 Prick eggplants in several places with the tip of a sharp knife – this prevents the eggplant from exploding during cooking. The best way to cook the eggplants is on a barbecue or under a hot grill for 30 minutes, turning them regularly so that they char evenly all over. This method creates a strong and authentic smoky flavour.

2 If grilling is not possible, preheat oven to 220°C. Place pricked eggplants on a tray and bake in the oven for 45 minutes or until very soft and shrivelled, and the skins have darkened and blistered. Set aside just until eggplants are cool enough to handle, then remove stems and peel off and discard the blistered skins.

3 Place eggplant flesh in a colander to drain for 10 minutes. Mash flesh with a fork to give a textured paste. This can also be done in a food processor, but it is best to pulse in short bursts so that the mixture retains some texture. Transfer mixture to a bowl and stir in tahini/labneh or thick yoghurt. Then add garlic and lemon juice, and season with salt and pepper to taste.

4 Serve in bowls drizzled with olive oil and garnish as desired. Serve with flatbread to scoop up the dip.

CHICKPEA PURÉE hummus & hummus bi tahini

Hummus is a soft, creamy chickpea purée that combines the tastes of sweet chickpea nuttiness, tinged with garlic and the tang of lemon juice. With the addition of tahini, this dip takes on a slightly earthy flavour and is then known as *hummus bi tahini*. Hummus, used as a spread or dip, is common throughout the Middle East, though recipes will vary from hand to hand.

While hummus is perhaps the most obvious recipe to include in a book of Middle Eastern recipes, I have included my version here because I believe that it is one of the hardest mixtures to make well. And, although hummus can be purchased ready-made, I choose to make my own as I enjoy having control over the blend of ingredients and the superior result this brings. I gain immeasurable pleasure from combining these few simple ingredients to achieve authentic hummus of incomparable taste, texture and freshness.

The key is to thoroughly soak the dried chickpeas overnight, then cook them until very tender (using canned chickpeas can make the mixture taste metallic). Always add freshly squeezed lemon juice, fresh garlic and tahini, as these tastes deteriorate quickly.

1 cup dried chickpeas, soaked overnight in plenty of cold water

4 cloves garlic, peeled

juice of 3 lemons

1/3–1/2 cup extra virgin olive oil

sea salt & freshly ground black pepper

3–4 tablespoons tahini (optional)

garnish options

extra virgin olive oil

sprinkling of ground paprika

a few olives

makes 2½ cups

1   Drain chickpeas and discard soaking liquid. Place chickpeas in a large saucepan and cover with plenty of water. Bring to the boil, then turn down heat, cover and simmer gently for 1 hour or until very tender. Drain chickpeas well and set aside to cool. Peeling the chickpeas at this stage is recommended, as peeled chickpeas result in a smoother-textured hummus. To do this, rub the chickpeas with your hands to remove and discard the outer skins.

2   Crush garlic in the bowl of a food processor, add chickpeas and pulse to chop. Add lemon juice and olive oil, and process well to combine into a smooth paste.

3   Add tahini at this stage to make hummus bi tahini, if desired. Or leave out the tahini for a clean-tasting chickpea purée.

4   Season hummus with salt and pepper to taste. Adjust amount of juice or oil to achieve desired taste and texture. Serve in bowls drizzled with olive oil and garnish as desired. Serve with plenty of flatbread to scoop up the dip.

RED PEPPER & WALNUT PASTE muhammara

Known as *muhammara* in Arabic, we ate this dip in Lebanon, Jordan, Syria and Turkey. Every version was subtly different but equally moreish. Some versions contained the addition of pomegranate molasses, others tomato paste, or a dash of yoghurt cheese to give a creamy richness. Turkish cooks will often add yoghurt for this same effect. Meaning 'made red', muhammara's red colouring relates to the rich red of the peppers combined with a sizeable inclusion of fiery red chilli or cayenne pepper.

3 red peppers
olive oil
1 cup walnuts, coarsely chopped
3 cloves garlic, crushed
½ teaspoon cayenne pepper or 1 red chilli, seeds removed, flesh coarsely chopped
juice of 1 lemon
3–4 tablespoons olive oil
sea salt & freshly ground black pepper

garnish options
extra virgin olive oil
a few olives
chopped fresh parsley

makes 2 cups

1 Preheat oven to 220°C. Remove the core, seeds and white membranes from peppers. Place halved red peppers in an oven pan, rub with a little olive oil and roast for 30 minutes, or until the skins blister and the flesh is soft.

2 Remove peppers to a bowl, cover with plastic wrap and set aside for 10–15 minutes so that the peppers sweat and the skins loosen. Once cool enough to handle, the skins can easily be slipped off and discarded.

3 Using a large mortar and pestle or a food processor, pound or process the red peppers to a pulp. Add walnuts, garlic, cayenne pepper or chilli and process to form a textured paste. Stir in oil and lemon juice, and season with salt and pepper to taste.

4 Spread the paste into a serving bowl, drizzle with olive oil and garnish as desired. Serve with warm flatbread to scoop up the dip.

(see photograph, page 21, front)

BROAD BEAN DIP bessara

This thick broad bean dip can be thinned with some of the reserved cooking liquid or stock and served as a soup. We regularly saw *bessara* sold as a street food in Egypt, ladled from large rounded urn-like pots that are evocatively heated over charcoal braziers.

1 cup dried broad beans or substitute
any brown bean
1 teaspoon baking soda
3 tablespoons olive oil
3 cloves garlic, peeled
juice of 1 lemon
⅓–½ cup olive oil
1 teaspoon ground cumin
1 teaspoon ground paprika
¼ teaspoon chilli powder
sea salt & freshly ground black pepper

serves 6

1 Place dried broad beans and baking soda in a large bowl, cover with plenty of cold water and leave to soak overnight.

2 Next day, drain beans and discard soaking liquid. Place beans in a saucepan with 3 tablespoons olive oil and garlic, and cover with plenty of fresh cold water. Bring to the boil, then simmer for 1 hour or until beans are very tender. Drain well, reserving cooking liquid if you wish to make bessara soup.

3 Purée beans in a blender, adding lemon juice and ⅓–½ cup oil to form a smooth paste. Season with cumin, paprika, chilli powder, salt and pepper to taste. Serve as a dip, garnished with a drizzle of olive oil.

4 Or, to make soup, return bean purée to a saucepan. Stir in reserved cooking liquid or stock and heat slowly. Garnish soup with extra lemon and cumin to taste.

spinach or cheese pastry triangles
fatayer bil-sabanegh / fatayer bil-qarish

These pretty little triangles of pastry are most traditionally filled with a sour spinach and pine nut mixture. The other option is a cheese and parsley combination, which is less common but equally tasty.

pastry

3 cups flour, plus extra for rolling out pastry

3 teaspoons baking powder

pinch salt

75g butter, melted

3 tablespoons olive oil

5–6 tablespoons cold water

egg wash

1 egg yolk beaten with 1 tablespoon milk, to glaze

makes 24

1 Sift flour with baking powder and salt into a bowl. Add butter and olive oil, and just enough water to form an elastic dough. Cover dough in bowl and set aside to rest for 1 hour. Meanwhile, prepare desired filling mixture (recipes follow).

2 On a lightly floured surface, roll out half the dough to 3mm thick. Use a pastry-cutter to cut out 9cm circles. Brush pastry edges with egg glaze and place a heaped teaspoonful of chosen filling in the centre of each circle. Fold three sides of each circle towards the centre to form a triangle-shaped pastry. To make enclosed pastries, seal the edges by pressing them together firmly, or leave pastries slightly open at the top, if preferred. Repeat the process with remaining pastry and filling.

3 Preheat oven to 200°C. Place pastry triangles on a baking tray lined with non-stick baking paper. Glaze pastry with egg wash and bake for 10–15 minutes, or until golden brown. Serve hot or warm.

spinach & pine nut filling

2 tablespoons olive oil
1 onion, finely diced
¼ cup pine nuts, toasted
500g spinach, washed, dried
& finely chopped
juice of 1 lemon
sea salt & freshly ground black pepper

1 Heat a frying pan, add olive oil and onion and cook over a moderate heat for 5–10 minutes until onion is softened but not coloured. Stir in pine nuts and cook for 2 minutes more to lightly toast nuts.

2 Add spinach and cook, stirring regularly until the spinach wilts. Add lemon juice and cook until this evaporates. Season with salt and pepper to taste. Cool mixture before using to fill pastry parcels.

(see photograph, page 26)

cheese filling

2 tablespoons olive oil
2 onions, finely diced
2 cloves garlic, chopped
½ teaspoon dried mint
¼ cup chopped fresh parsley
2 eggs, lightly beaten
2 tablespoons milk
1 cup labneh (see page 120)
250g feta cheese, crumbled
sea salt & freshly ground black pepper

1 Heat a frying pan, add olive oil, onion and garlic and cook over a moderate heat for 5–10 minutes until onion is softened but not coloured. Add herbs and cook for a minute more. Transfer mixture to a bowl.

2 Beat in eggs, milk, labneh and feta until mixture is well combined. Season with pepper to taste, and salt if necessary, bearing in mind that the cheese mixture is already quite salty.

LAMB SAMBOUSEK

Discovered during the Crusades, it is believed that these Levantine meat pastries later inspired the development of meat pies and Cornish pasties in Britain. The pastries are more commonly fried but I prefer to bake them in the oven so that the paper-thin pastry is not so laden with fat. The choice is yours as either cooking method works well.

pastry

2 cups plain flour

1 teaspoon sea salt

⅔ cup cold water to mix

extra flour for kneading & rolling

1 egg beaten with 1 tablespoon water, to seal pastries

sunflower oil for deep-frying

1 Sift flour and salt into a bowl. Add just enough water to form an elastic dough, mixing the dough with a knife. Remove from the bowl and knead on a lightly floured surface for 5 minutes until smooth. Return dough to bowl, cover with plastic wrap and refrigerate for 30 minutes to rest.

2 On a lightly floured surface, roll out dough to 3mm thick. Use a pastry-cutter to cut out 9cm circles. Place a tablespoonful of lamb filling (recipe follows) in the centre of each circle. Dampen edges with a little beaten egg and fold the pastry circle in half to cover the filling and form a crescent shape. Press edges with your fingers to seal. Crimp with a fork or by making tight overlapping folds with the pastry around the edge. Repeat the process with remaining pastry and filling.

3 Heat oil to 170°C or test temperature by adding a crust of bread – if it bubbles and gently turns golden brown the oil is at the correct temperature. Cook pastries in batches of 4–5 at a time, until golden brown. Remove with a slotted spoon and drain on paper towels. Serve warm.

4 Alternatively, if you do not wish to deep-fry the pastries, place them on baking trays lined with non-stick baking paper. Preheat oven to 200°C and bake pastries for 15 minutes, or until golden brown.

lamb filling

1 tablespoon olive oil

1 onion, finely diced

2 cloves garlic, chopped

375g lean lamb mince

3 tablespoons toasted pine nuts

2 tablespoons chopped fresh mint
or 1 teaspoon dried mint

1 teaspoon ground cinnamon

¼ teaspoon each ground allspice
& chilli powder

juice of 1 lemon

sea salt & freshly ground black pepper

makes 24

1 Heat a frying pan, add oil, onion and garlic and cook over a medium-high heat for 5 minutes until onion is softened and golden brown. Add lamb mince and cook until browned, breaking up the mince mixture as it cooks. Drain off any excess fat.

2 Add pine nuts, mint, spices and lemon juice and cook for 2–3 minutes more. Season with salt and pepper to taste. Cool mixture before using to fill pastry parcels.

(see photograph, page 27)

herbal trinity coriander, parsley, mint

Herb stalls flourish in the old medina. Valued for the powerfully fragrant and fresh clean tastes herbs add to dishes, generous use is made of them in Middle Eastern cooking. While many different herbs can be found throughout the regions, coriander, mint and parsley tend to predominate in the kitchen.

Coriander may be pulverised into a pungent sauce or used to stuff whole fish. Bunches of perfumed mint are served as part of a mezze spread, or the leaves may be used to form a refreshing tea infusion. Flat-leaf parsley is typically chopped and may be added to myriad dishes – perhaps beaten with eggs to form the central flavouring of an Arabic omelette or, indeed, eaten whole like a salad leaf, in all its natural glory.

Tabbouleh is an excellent example of a salad made mainly of herbs. True tabbouleh is essentially parsley salad bound with a little burghul wheat, rather than burghul salad tossed with a little parsley – as often erroneously recreated in the West.

One day in Lebanon, while we were exploring the souk in Tripoli, known as the capital of Northern Lebanon, we are invited into a domestic kitchen to taste authentic homemade tabbouleh. This souk is a vast entanglement of covered alleyways teeming with life, food stalls, music, living crafts and local craftspeople – wood-turners, olive oil soap-makers, potters, goldsmiths and tailors. I'm enveloped by a prevailing fragrance that smells like the dust of the past mingled with shades of mint, spices, rose water, brewing coffee.

Within the narrow lanes of the souk it is easy to feel confused by the displays and all the cacophony of present-day Tripoli. Just as we begin to feel we have lost our way, a stranger stops us to warmly say in English, 'Welcome to Lebanon'. As the only tourists in the souk we are as much a curiosity to the locals as the chaos of the souk is to us. 'You come to my home for looking and I make you tabbouleh! Okay?' the stranger says. We find ourselves agreeing to this slightly disarming but irresistible offer from our new friend, whose name is Ragat.

Armed with an address, we travel out of the centre of town, past industrial estates and high into the hills outside Tripoli. When we finally arrive at a simple village nestled under an ancient and imposing stone-walled mosque, the Muslim call to prayer reverberates out from the loudspeakers of the mosque for all to hear.

The whole village is keen to welcome us – at one stage, twenty-nine of Ragat's closest relatives are crammed into one small room, and excited groups of children have climbed the walls outside for a better view of us, their honoured guests.

We sit at an old wooden table in a rudimentary kitchen where we are offered simple renditions of traditional local dishes. We taste Ragat's tabbouleh – a lush parsley rendition united with a little burghul wheat and tomato, and dressed with a liberal amount of lemon juice. We eat with our right hands, as is the time-honoured tradition, using lettuce leaves to scoop up the tabbouleh.

The secret of authentic tabbouleh lies in the way the ingredients are prepared and combined. The parsley and mint leaves must be chopped by hand so that they remain crisp and only sustain minimal bruising. The amount of burghul wheat added does vary according to local, family or personal tradition. Ragat learned from her mother to use only a smattering amount so that parsley remains the dominant flavour.

Later, we are entertained in the most decorated room in the house, a sofa-lined living room where we are invited to smoke the hubbly bubbly water pipe and drink tiny cups of perfumed Arabic coffee. It is rude to refuse, so we all join in. Then we are expected to dance, which is a tiny bit disconcerting. Men, and then women, must dance separately. So I dance in the middle of the room, to the admiration of the others, and to the accompaniment of improvised rhythmic drumming – in this case, on an upturned plastic bucket, along with clapping and vibrant ululating sounds from the women.

Our energetic dancing is followed by a respectful tour of the ancient mosque next door before we are given a hearty send-off into the moonless, inky darkness of the night.

LEBANESE FATTOUSH

This humble but character-filled Lebanese bread salad is dedicated to my wonderful Lebanese great-grandfather, Samuel Saleem Bishara, whom I never met but oh so wish I had. In Lebanon, we tasted many different versions of this salad. As with most home-cooked dishes, the recipe will vary from village to village and even from person to person.

Purslane is a herbal salad leaf that is traditionally added (and is my favourite addition), but I have suggested other salad greens if purslane is not available. There are other variables as well. Most often the pita bread is fried but I prefer to bake it for a less oily consistency. Some cooks add radishes or spring onions; some will omit the lettuce, as desired. In Northern Lebanon, pomegranate molasses is often added to the dressing. And it is also interesting to note that in Syria, fattoush may be made with the addition of fried eggplant.

Sumac, a pungent, astringent spice ground from the crimson berries of a decorative bush peculiar to the Middle East, adds an important flavour component to fattoush, though don't worry if you cannot find it, the salad will still be delicious.

2 large rounds of pita bread

olive oil

2 Lebanese cucumbers, rinsed

8 medium-sized vine-ripened tomatoes

1 red onion, peeled or a bunch of spring onions

1 cup purslane, lamb's lettuce (*mache*), watercress, rocket leaves or diced iceberg lettuce

¼ cup chopped fresh parsley

¼ cup chopped fresh coriander

¼ cup chopped fresh mint

sea salt & freshly ground black pepper

2 teaspoons sumac

lebanese lemon dressing

3 cloves garlic, crushed

⅓ cup lemon juice

¼ cup extra virgin olive oil

serves 6

1. Preheat oven to 180°C. Brush pita bread with olive oil and spread on a baking tray. Bake for 10–15 minutes or until golden and crisp. Remove, cool, then break or shatter into small fragments.

2. Dice cucumbers, tomatoes and red onion and combine in a bowl with lettuce and herbs. Season well with plenty of salt and pepper.

3. Blend dressing ingredients together. Pour dressing over the salad ingredients and toss well to coat. Lastly toss in the toasted pita bread pieces so that they remain crisp.

4. Sprinkle with sumac, if available.

ORIENTAL SALAD baladi

It is interesting to note that people from the Middle East consider themselves Oriental, but when Westerners think of the Orient they are more likely to think of the Far East. This self-definition is demonstrated on menus where dishes often have Oriental names. This Oriental salad is a classic example, though it does also go by the name of *baladi*. We ate this simple salad many times, often as an accompaniment to meat kebabs. The very generous executive chef on our Egyptian cruise boat, *Sun Boat IV*, gave this particular recipe to me.

5 medium-sized vine-ripened tomatoes, seeds removed

2 Lebanese cucumbers, seeds removed

I red onion, peeled

3 radishes

I green pepper, core & seeds removed

½ cup chopped fresh parsley

juice of 3 lemons

4 tablespoons extra virgin olive oil

I clove garlic, crushed

I teaspoon toasted ground cumin

sea salt & freshly ground black pepper

serves 4–6

1 Coarsely dice tomatoes, cucumber, onion, radishes and green pepper and place in a bowl.

2 Combine with remaining ingredients. Season generously with salt and pepper to taste, and toss well.

34

TABBOULEH

It is a common misconception that tabbouleh is a burghul salad made with the addition of herbs. In fact, a true tabbouleh is made in a ratio of substantially more parsley to grain. We particularly enjoyed this authentic preparation made for us by Ragat in her home in the hills just outside of Tripoli (Lebanon) — here is her special recipe.

¼ cup fine burghul

2 large bunches fresh flat-leaf parsley, coarsely chopped

1 small bunch fresh mint, coarsely chopped

200g firm vine-ripened tomatoes, finely diced

3 spring onions, finely sliced

juice of 3 lemons

¼ cup extra virgin olive oil

sea salt & freshly ground black pepper

lettuce leaves to serve

serves 4–6

1 Rinse burghul in several changes of cold water, then drain well and place in a large salad bowl.

2 Add remaining ingredients, season generously with salt and pepper to taste and toss well (traditionally this is done by hand). Taste and adjust seasoning, if necessary.

3 Tabbouleh is often served with lettuce leaves, which are used to cup mouthfuls of the salad, like edible spoons.

YEMENI ZHOUG

Zhoug is a hot chilli and coriander relish, used for flavouring soups and stews or served as a dip for bread. Originating in Yemen, zhoug is now also popular in Israel.

4 dried red chillies

4 cardamom pods, seeds removed

1 teaspoon caraway seeds

8 cloves garlic, coarsely chopped

1 cup chopped fresh coriander leaves

3 tablespoons olive oil

sea salt & freshly ground black pepper

makes 1 cup

1 Cover chillies with boiling water and set aside to soak for 2 hours. Drain and coarsely chop chillies, then pound in a mortar and pestle or food processor.

2 Grind cardamon and caraway seeds to a powder. Add ground seeds, chopped garlic and coriander to chillies and pound or process together to form a rough-textured purée. Blend in oil and season with salt and pepper.

3 Pour into a sterilised jar and seal well. This relish will last for 3–4 weeks if stored in the fridge.

PARSLEY OMELETTE *kuku*

Essentially this is a parsley omelette, which is known as *kuku* in Persian cuisine, or as *eggah* in some other countries of the Middle East, such as Egypt. Arabic omelettes are different in texture to French omelettes, being more firm than fluffy, and could be compared more favourably to Spanish tortilla. To serve, a large kuku may be cut into wedges or small squares. Alternatively, the mixture can be used to make parsley fritters by dropping spoonfuls in a hot oiled pan and frying until golden brown on both sides.

2–3 tablespoons olive oil
1 onion, finely diced
3 cloves garlic, chopped
6 eggs, lightly beaten
2 teaspoons dried mint, ground
1 cup finely chopped fresh flat-leaf parsley
sea salt & freshly ground black pepper
olive oil for frying
sprigs of fresh parsley to garnish

serves 6

1 Heat a 22cm ovenproof omelette pan or frying pan, add 2 tablespoons oil and the onion and cook over a medium heat for 10 minutes, stirring frequently until onion is softened but not coloured. Add garlic and cook for 1 minute. Remove to a plate to cool.

2 In a bowl, combine beaten eggs with cooled onion mixture, mint and parsley, and season well with salt and pepper.

3 Heat a frying pan, add a film of oil, then pour in egg mixture. Cook over a gentle heat for 15–20 minutes or until the mixture is set. To finish, lightly brown the top under a preheated grill. Turn kuku out onto a plate and slice to serve.

4 For fritters, heat a large non-stick frying pan with enough oil to shallow-fry fritters. Cook tablespoonful lots of the mixture for 1–2 minutes or until each one has set, then turn fritters over to lightly brown the other side. Remove to drain on paper towels. Serve warm with a bowl of olives and some warm flatbread.

37

COURGETTES WITH MINT tabbakh rubu

The Lebanese call this vivacious dish *tabbakh rubu*, which means 'the spirit of the cook'. It is true that mint and courgette makes for a lively combination. Lebanese courgettes are very pale in colour and appear to be almost seedless. They may appear insipid in comparison to the darker variety of courgette but they have a wonderfully delicate, sweet flavour.

750g small courgettes, trimmed
3 cloves garlic
I teaspoon dried mint
3 tablespoons chopped fresh mint
sea salt & freshly ground black pepper
¼ cup olive oil

serves 6

1 Preheat oven to 200°C. Thickly slice courgettes on the diagonal and place in a bowl.

2 Pound garlic, mint and a little salt in a mortar and pestle or food processor to form a smooth paste, then blend in oil. Pour this mixture over courgettes, season with salt and pepper and toss well.

3 Transfer courgettes to a casserole dish and bake for 40–45 minutes, tossing once during cooking, until tender and lightly golden brown.

OLIVE & PARSLEY SALAD

The bite of briny olives contrasted with the freshness of parsley and lemon makes this unusual salad combination very refreshing. A salad like this works well as a mezze dish, and can play the part of palate cleanser when nibbled between richer tastes and textures.

2 cups quality black olives,
pitted & coarsely chopped
2 cups packed fresh flat-leaf parsley leaves
I small red onion, finely sliced
juice of 4 lemons
2 tablespoons extra virgin olive oil
sea salt & freshly ground black pepper

serves 6

1 Place olives, parsley and onion in a salad bowl. Sprinkle with lemon juice and drizzle with olive oil.

2 Toss well. Taste and adjust seasoning with salt and pepper and toss again.

38

A stroll through the spice souk stimulates all my senses. Tins overflow with brightly coloured powders, and nose-tingling scents mingle together in dizzying profusion. There are neatly tied bundles of twisted twigs, tactile clumps of bark and roots, and baskets or open sacks of plant seeds, leaves and blushing pink rosebuds. The air is dense with robust flavours of cardamom, fennel, chilli and turmeric that tickle my taste-buds.

Spices have a long history in these parts. Exotic spices were so highly valued by early traders that the sea routes connecting trade between the East and the West became known as the Spice Routes. Traders returned from the Far East, through Indonesia, via India and Africa, with cargoes of these mysterious substances that continue to be used in spiritual, medicinal and culinary practices today.

From early times, spices have been burnt like incense in religious ceremonies. Cardamom seeds are added to coffee to give this drink a distinctly Arabic taste, or chewed as a digestive and breath freshener. And in cooking, familiar spices are used in unexpected ways. For instance, cinnamon, especially favoured in Turkish and Egyptian cooking, is used to enhance both sweet and savoury foods.

In Oman, I am excited to find deep within Muscat's spice souk the curious resinous substances of frankincense and mastic. Frankincense, the sap of a strange, leafless tree that grows exclusively in the desert of southern Oman, looks like pale amber-coloured toffee. Commonly burnt over hot coals to perfume the room, frankincense can also be eaten like chewing gum and is reputed to be good for the digestion. I buy a small amount to try. It tastes aromatic, a little like eucalyptus or pine needles, but soon becomes glued to my teeth where it lingers for some hours as a reminder of the experience.

Mastic, a similar product, is formed from the sap of the lentisk tree, a species of wild Eastern Mediterranean pine. Mastic can also be chewed but is usually ground into a dusty powder and used to flavour various sweets and pastries.

The Middle East is also a home to saffron. Worth more than its weight in gold, saffron is the result of the painstaking work of women who gather the stigmas from thousands of crocus flowers in an early-morning harvest of legendary dimensions. Such labour-intensive production demands a high price, but fortunately, because saffron is very potent, a tiny amount goes a long way. A pinch of saffron will richly flavour food with its unique earthy spiciness and infuse any dish with a golden hue.

The particular species of autumn-flowering crocus that yields saffron threads grows wild in Iran. Iranian saffron is not considered the best in the world – Spanish saffron, introduced by the Arabs, is generally thought to be superior. Nonetheless, Iranian saffron is good, and any dish infused with this prized spice will be suitably enriched.

Another distinctive spice, sumac, is used in the cooking of many Middle Eastern countries, such as Jordan, Syria, Iran, Iraq and Turkey, but most especially in Lebanon. It is a pungent, astringent powder ground from the reddish purple berries of a decorative bush peculiar to the region. Steeped in water, sumac is used in the same way as, or in place of, lemon juice. It may be sprinkled over fish or salads to add flavour and is also one of the key three ingredients in the spice mix known as za'atar.

The tradition of using multiple spice mixes remains strong in these countries. Astute blending and careful application of spices to highlight flavours make many Middle Eastern dishes alluringly perfumed and delicious. Different countries or regions have particular spice blends or preferences and many spices are favoured for their aromatics rather than heat.

In the Gulf States, however, I notice more chilli-hot dishes and a strong culinary influence from India, which of course is just across the Arabian Sea from Iran, Bahrain, the United Arab Emirates, Oman and the Yemen.

We eat lunch in Muscat at a local restaurant where firstly we are told we must sit in a segregated dining area, as here no woman can eat in the same room as men. Settled in what is called the 'family room', we eat a deliciously simple *biryani* of fish. This is a highly spiced saffron curry and basmati rice dish typically found in India but now a staple of the Omani kitchen.

BAHARAT

Baharat is a specialised spice blend commonly used in the cooking of the Persian Gulf states and Iraq.

2 teaspoons each black pepper & paprika

2 teaspoons each cumin & coriander seeds, toasted & ground

1 teaspoon ground cinnamon

½ teaspoon each ground cardamom, cloves & nutmeg

makes ¼ cup

1 Combine spices and store in a sealed jar. Use within 1 month.

ZA'ATAR

Za'atar is the Arabic name for dried thyme, but it also refers to a mixture of dried thyme combined with sesame seeds and the powdered sour berry known as sumac. This za'atar mix is commonly used as a topping for flatbread, which is often eaten for breakfast or as a street-food snack (see page 135).

½ cup dried thyme

¼ cup sumac

¼ cup lightly toasted sesame seeds

makes 1 cup

1 Combine all ingredients. Store in a sealed jar and use within 1 month.

42

DUKKAH

Dukkah is a spice mixture of Egyptian origin. Rather like wine, each recipe demonstrates the maker's personality and will vary from place to place and from family to family. Dukkah can be eaten as a spicy dip for bread, which is first dipped in olive oil. I have found that it also works well as a seasoning to sprinkle over other dishes like roast chicken, fish or vegetables.

½ cup hazelnuts
¼ cup toasted sesame seeds
I tablespoon toasted cumin seeds
I tablespoon toasted coriander seeds
I teaspoon paprika
½ teaspoon freshly ground black pepper
I teaspoon sea salt
olive oil & flatbread to serve

makes ¾ cup

1 Preheat oven to 180°C. Place hazelnuts in an oven pan and roast for 20 minutes or until golden brown. Transfer from the oven tray to a clean tea towel. Fold tea towel to enclose nuts and rub vigorously to loosen skins. Pick out clean nuts and discard skins.

2 Place hazelnuts with all the toasted seeds and remaining ingredients in a spice mill or food processor and pulse to grind together — take care not to pulverise the mixture or it will turn into a paste.

3 Place dukkah in a serving bowl. Dip a fragment of bread first into olive oil and then into dukkah. Best used freshly made, dukkah can be stored in an airtight container in the fridge for up to a week if necessary.

persian gulf prawn curry

When visiting the Gulf States I noticed a strong culinary influence coming from India, which of course is just across the Arabian sea from Iran, Oman and Yemen, and around the corner (metaphorically speaking) from places like Bahrain, Kuwait and the United Arab Emirates. Chilli, fresh ginger, limes, tamarind and spices are also typically included in dishes of this region.

3 tablespoons vegetable oil,
such as sunflower oil

2 onions, chopped

2 tablespoons freshly grated root ginger

3 cloves garlic, crushed

1 teaspoon prepared baharat spice
blend (see page 42)

½ teaspoon chilli powder

2 teaspoons turmeric powder

1 cinnamon stick

2 dried limes (or substitute the pared
rind of 1 fresh lime)

400g can chopped tomatoes

¼ cup tamarind water (or substitute
lemon or lime juice)

1 cup cold water

700g peeled king prawns, deveined

sea salt & freshly ground black pepper

steamed basmati rice to serve

fresh lime halves to garnish

serves 4

1 Heat a large frying pan, add oil and onions and cook over a gentle heat for 10 minutes until onions are softened but not coloured. Add ginger, garlic and spices and fry for 1 minute to release flavours. Add dried limes.

2 Stir in tomatoes, tamarind water and 1 cup cold water. Bring to the boil, then simmer for 10 minutes to reduce and concentrate flavours.

3 Place prawns in sauce, cover pan and simmer for 10 minutes until cooked through. Serve with steamed basmati rice and fresh lime halves.

44

OMANI SPICE-MARINATED TUNA

Seafood – especially prawns, lobster, game fish like tuna, and a plethora of other fish – is the pride of the Omani kitchen. One balmy evening, as we sat on the terrace flooded with moonlight, we enjoyed this dish fresh from the barbecue of the Hyatt Hotel in Muscat.

4 x 150g portions fresh tuna
½ teaspoon chilli flakes
½ teaspoon crushed coriander seeds
1 teaspoon ground paprika
juice of 2 limes
3 tablespoons olive oil
sea salt & freshly ground black pepper
2 tablespoons chopped fresh coriander

serves 4

1 Place tuna in a deep, flat ceramic dish. Combine spices with lime juice and olive oil and pour over tuna, turning tuna to evenly coat pieces in marinade. Cover and marinate for 1 hour in the fridge.

2 Remove tuna to room temperature when ready to cook. Season on both sides with salt and pepper.

3 Heat a barbecue or char-grill pan. Cook tuna for 2–4 minutes on each side, depending on thickness of flesh, until the outer thirds have turned pale but the centre third remains rare. Remove to a serving dish and scatter with fresh coriander.

SPICED MEATBALLS OR MINCED MEAT KEBABS kofta

These minced meat kebabs have a special velvety texture. The inclusion of soaked bread in the mix creates this smooth, soft and moist texture, and also acts to bind the mixture so that the *kofta* do not fall apart when cooked. Kofta may be moulded into long sausage shapes onto skewers — these are sometimes called *kefta*, depending on the country. Kofta can also be formed into meatballs and fried or baked in a tomato sauce. Balls of kofta sometimes appear in soups too.

48

2 slices stale white bread,
crusts removed, roughly torn

⅓ cup milk

I teaspoon each ground cumin,
coriander, paprika & cinnamon

½ teaspoon allspice

650g minced lamb (or beef)

½ onion, grated or very finely chopped

3 cloves garlic, crushed

¼ cup chopped fresh coriander,
mint or parsley

sea salt & freshly ground black pepper

olive oil for frying

serves 4

1 Place torn bread in a bowl, pour over milk and leave to soak and soften. Toast the combined spices in a dry skillet for a few minutes until fragrant, then remove to a plate.

2 In a bowl, combine soaked bread and milk, toasted spices, lamb, onion, garlic, coriander, mint or parsley. Pound together with your hand against the bowl until amalgamated and smooth (this will help the mixture hold together when cooked).

3 Season mixture well with salt and pepper, then fry a small piece to check seasoning, and adjust seasoning if necessary.

4 Divide the mixture into 20 equal portions. With damp hands (to stop the mixture sticking to your hands), roll each portion into a ball. Heat a frying pan over a medium heat. Add a little oil and pan-fry meatballs in 2–3 batches for 5–7 minutes, turning to brown all over. Drain on paper towels.

5 Kofta can be reheated in the oven as is or coated in a simple tomato sauce. Or, mould mixture onto skewers and cook on a barbecue or under a preheated grill for 3–4 minutes on each side. Serve traditionally with pita bread and salad and *caçik* (see page 125).

SPICED CHICKEN KEBABS WITH CREAMY GARLIC SAUCE
shish tawouk with toum

Shish kebabs are one of the most common dishes found throughout the Middle East. This chicken version, while succulent and flavoursome, is lifted to majestic heights by the addition of dollops of *toum*, a remarkable garlic sauce accompaniment. This sauce transforms any dish it accompanies into something quite sublime.

700g boneless & skinless chicken meat
(breast & thigh meat)

6 cloves garlic, crushed

½ teaspoon ground allspice

½ teaspoon ground cinnamon

pinch chilli powder

juice of 1 lemon

2 tablespoons olive oil

sea salt & freshly ground black pepper

pita bread to serve

serves 4

1 Cut chicken meat into 1cm cubes. In a bowl, combine garlic and spices with lemon juice and olive oil to make a marinade. Place cubed chicken in the marinade and mix well. Cover and refrigerate for 2 hours, turning chicken in the marinade 2–3 times.

2 Preheat a barbecue or grill. Thread cubes of chicken onto 12 metal skewers, evenly distributing pieces between skewers. Season with salt and pepper.

3 Grill for 2–3 minutes on each side or until browned all over and cooked through. Lay cooked kebabs on opened pita bread to serve hot with creamy garlic sauce (recipe follows) on the side.

CREAMY GARLIC SAUCE toum

Toum is a pungent garlic sauce emulsified with olive oil. It has the same remarkably creamy, almost fluffy texture of aïoli (garlic mayonnaise) but amazingly does not include egg yolks. Use toum as a dipping sauce for grilled chicken kebabs or to baste chicken while grilling. At first I was very cautious of this potent garlic sauce, but once I tried this slightly mysterious mixture I found it unforgettable and addictive.

5 cloves garlic

¼ teaspoon sea salt

2 tablespoons lemon juice

½ cup olive oil

1 tablespoon water

makes 1 cup

1 Place garlic, salt and lemon juice in the bowl of a food processor and process to purée.

2 Gradually blend in oil – the mixture will emulsify like mayonnaise forming a thick, creamy paste.

3 Finally, blend in water. Store in the fridge.

SHAWARMA

Shawarma can be found on nearly every street corner in most Arab countries. The distinctive cones consist of layer upon layer of spice-marinated meat (usually lamb, but sometimes beef or chicken) tightly packed on a spit. The spit is placed vertically in front of an open flame or gas fire and the meat is turned as it cooks. The shawarma chef takes his sharp knife in hand and shaves off paper-thin slices of cooked meat, which drop into a waiting tray below. The cooked meat, along with salad and tahini or garlic sauce, is placed in a pocket of pita bread.

It is hard to make homemade shawarma unless you've got an upright spit and vertical shawarma cooking fire and that is why it is not normally made at home. But for those who wish to try, here is a recipe that will give you authentic flavours.

marinade

3 tablespoons lemon juice

1 tablespoon cider vinegar

2 tablespoons extra virgin olive oil

4 cloves garlic, crushed

2 tablespoons onion, finely grated

¼ teaspoon cayenne pepper

½ teaspoon each ground coriander, cinnamon, cloves, nutmeg & allspice

½ teaspoon freshly ground black pepper

1 teaspoon sea salt

500g lamb (or beef or skinless chicken breasts), thinly sliced

pita bread to serve

tahini sauce (see page 80) or toum (see page 51) to serve

oriental salad to serve (see page 34)

serves 4

1 Combine all marinade ingredients in a large, deep, flat ceramic dish. Add strips of meat and toss well to evenly coat in marinade. Cover and refrigerate to marinate overnight.

2 Bring meat to room temperature for 30 minutes before cooking. Preheat a grill on high. Place marinated meat and marinade in a large oven pan and cook under the grill for 15 minutes, turning meat once, until browned.

3 Serve strips of cooked meat in pita bread, topped with thinned *tahini taratour* (tahini sauce) or toum and Oriental salad.

PETRA, JORDAN

We decide to hire a car and drive from Amman in Jordan to the country's most famous historic site, Petra. We take the quickest route from Amman, a three-hour drive south on the Desert Highway. We pass through a raw rock-scape of desert, broken only by some industry, the occasional small settlement and road signs letting us know that we are so many kilometres from the Iraqi border or from Saudi Arabia.

We're halfway there now and in need of a refreshment stop, which appears, literally, in the middle of nowhere. By the side of the road, under the flapping awning of a handcart, we are surprised to see two tall and now-familiar Arabic coffee-pots letting off steam into the desert air. Likewise, the man behind the coffee-pots seems somewhat baffled by our arrival. We pass a short but pleasant time, sipping coffee and making shy conversation with the use of sign language. Then, fuelled with caffeine, we continue our drive to Petra.

We arrive at lunchtime. After a quick meal at a hotel near the visitors' centre to sustain us, we set off in search of this famous lost city. We buy entrance passes, grab maps and start walking. From the entrance, a track leads us to the *siq*, a slender passageway through a gorge that will take us into Petra. Once inside, the path narrows in parts, or suddenly widens to reveal ghostly, eroded frescoes, votive niches, and other faded decorative elements etched into the formless rock. Above

head-height, we are fascinated to see visible traces of original water canals – a refined aqueduct system dug into the rock that once brought water into Petra.

The soaring red sandstone walls on each side of us form dark purple shadows at ground level. With the turn of each corner, our anticipation builds until a kilometre or so along the path, and just when we least expect it, a final corner reveals a glimpse of what is to come. A portion of Al-Khaneh, The Treasury, shows through the narrow opening at the end of the crevice, dramatically framed by the cliffs closing in about us. Shining rose-pink in the brilliant sunlight, in contrast to the slanting gloom shrouding our pathway, this vision is literally like a light at the end of a tunnel.

I find it tempting to linger in the shadows, to let my eyes become re-acquainted with the harsh light and to allow the breathtaking image of The Treasury's façade to expand into view, slowly. As I pause to take a photograph, I find a camel perfectly positioned in the centre of the frame, as if carefully placed to complete my own picture-postcard image.

Even on this, my second visit, I am left awestruck once again as I rediscover this hidden desert kingdom. Nothing can prepare you for the majesty of Petra, in spite of seeing an abundance of images in books and brochures.

We leave the chasm now. Strong sunlight shows all the details of The Treasury's massive and elaborately carved façade, which depicts gods and goddesses and mythological figures. We marvel, as all visitors to Petra do, at the sheer size of this structure and the ingenuity of its early construction.

Petra is a monument to the visionary thinking of the Nabateans (an early Arab people) and to their skills of architecture, stone-carving and hydraulic engineering. It was they who transformed a desert of hostile rock into Petra – a city furnished with temples, banquet halls, Roman theatres, monasteries, houses, roads, baths and a complex water system, the ruins of which we see today. At one stage, this first-century metropolis dominated the trade routes of ancient Arabia and was the central hub of the spice trade.

Once the Romans took control of the trade routes, the decline of Petra began. Archaeologists believe a massive earthquake finally forced its inhabitants to abandon the city. Petra remained hidden to the outside world until rediscovered in 1812 by the Swiss explorer, Johann Ludwig Burckhardt.

Suddenly we hear the cries of a camel owner beckoning us. 'You must ride my fully optioned Bedouin Ferrari,' he insists, to our amusement. Kicking up dust from the mouth of As-Siq, through the bowels of the ravine and back again, are specialised forms of local transport – their owners calling out for clients to ride horseback, donkeys, or (only possibly more comfortable) in horse-drawn carriages. A donkey is described as a 'BMW taxi', and an open carriage as having 'air-conditioning'.

However, we choose to keep walking, for the time being. The Treasury is only the first of Petra's secrets – we have much more to discover and this is best done on foot. Dotted along our path we encounter Bedouin women selling beads and so-called ancient artifacts, their faces engraved with unusually faded tribal tattoos. Children start life within Petra selling postcards

from a very young age. It is a hard way to eke out a living.

We move on through the Street of Façades, past many tombs to the amphitheatre, which can hold 7000 people. An open space leads us to the city's heart, the Colonnaded Street, once a marketplace.

Access to the monastery and many of the tomb sites (there are over 500 scattered throughout Petra) involves a long and strenuous trek, but as it is near closing time we must turn back. Our late start means we are almost the last to leave and now it feels like we are the only people here. It's an eerie feeling to have Petra to ourselves.

Instead of retracing our steps on foot, we decide to take one of the Bedouin taxis with air-con back to our starting point. We squeeze into the dilapidated carriage and are jostled along, serenaded by the sound of metal horseshoes clopping against solid rock. Only traces of the original paved road remain along the siq and so our ride is a little rough – and a little scary when our driver starts racing through narrow chasms, literally competing with another carriage to reach the finish line.

On our drive back to Amman, I recall another excursion that I enjoyed on a previous visit to this region.

I had reached the Dead Sea from the Israeli side, but it can also be accessed from Jordan, and is a short day trip from Amman. The Dead Sea is actually a lake and is the lowest point on earth at 400 metres below sea level. The lake's water has such high salinity that bathers become suspended in the concentrated solution – a sensation that feels quite bizarre. And the healing, health and cosmetic benefits of the lake's mud are expounded by local health spas.

I wasn't keen to smother myself with Dead Sea mud, but as I edged into the shallows I discovered that it is possible to stand up in the thick, salty water. However, once I tried to immerse myself, I found my body was incredibly buoyant. It's literally impossible to sink into the water's depths, which is a relief really, because the highly salty, mineral-packed brew feels dense and slimy. It was strange to see people floating on top of the water, as if lying on invisible airbeds. I resorted to doing what all tourists do and read a newspaper while afloat, reclining on the thick saline solution.

Golden saffron-stained grains of rice, dotted with nuts and dried fruits glistening like precious jewels, are heaped on a silver tray and laid on the table before us. We are in an Iranian restaurant enjoying this distinctly Persian dish. Persia is thought by many to be the mother of Middle Eastern cuisine, though others contest that it is Lebanon, Syria or Turkey. Nevertheless, no matter what Middle Eastern country you look to, rice is vital to the cuisine and forms the basis on which many meals are built.

Steamed rice is an excellent companion to fish, meat and vegetable stews, and kebabs. And when combined with an assortment of other ingredients, such as dried fruit and nuts, lentils, beans and chickpeas, rice becomes a complete meal in itself.

Middle Eastern recipes also warmly embrace pulses. Two well-known dishes based on the humble chickpea are hummus and falafel. There is immeasurable pleasure to be gained from handcrafting a batch of homemade hummus to achieve all the desirable taste and textural characteristics that this authentic dish should hold. Advance preparation is important and this involves soaking the dried chickpeas overnight. Then the chickpeas must be cooked until meltingly tender. I peel off their skins, if I feel inclined. Finally, I blend the soft chickpeas with chopped garlic, salt, tahini and a plentiful amount of olive oil and freshly squeezed lemon juice to make a simple dish with ancient qualities.

Falafels are best when freshly made and cooked. We watch a busy falafel maker in Sidon, southern Lebanon. He stands beside a bowl of special falafel mixture – each cook has their own secret recipe. He dips in a metal instrument, like an ice-cream scoop, which forms the moist chickpea mixture into a ball. Then with a flick of the handle, the ball drops into the vat of bubbling hot oil, frying into a wonderfully crisp snack. Smiling, he hands me one to try. Fragrant with cumin and parsley, it is crunchy on the outside and delectably moist inside.

Another protein-packed and nutritional ingredient of Arabic cooking is the *fava* bean. On the street-food stalls of Egypt we find famous dishes based on these beans – distinctive pots of fava beans cooking over braziers and the common breakfast dish of *ful medames*, a salad of broad beans served garnished with egg, parsley and spring onions.

Ground parboiled wheat, known as burghul, is widely used to make breads, tabbouleh and pilafs, or kneaded with meat to make *kibbeh* – the national dish of Lebanon. The word kibbeh comes from the verb meaning 'to form into a ball'. The basic ingredients for kibbeh are burghul and the freshest tender pink lamb. These two simple components are pounded together by hand until they take on a smooth velvety texture – a time-consuming operation. Balls of the mixture are then shaped into different forms, such as patties, ovals or domes. Kibbeh may be served raw or cooked, filled and fried like rissoles, or baked in one layer. And sometimes kibbeh appears in certain soups or sauces, such as kibbeh cooked in yoghurt.

High in the Lebanese Mountains near the town of B'sharre, we stop at the River Roc Café for lunch. The owner insists I try his version of kibbeh. I'm told this particular dome-shaped kibbeh is stuffed with 'white meat' and I am directed to eat it quickly. The sun is shining brightly as we gaze out over the valley, however, the temperature is still icy cold. Cutting open the kibbeh releases the filling, which sets quickly on the plate. I discover that white meat is simply fat.

Kousheri, another historic Middle Eastern dish, has today become the fast food of Egypt. A combination of pasta, rice and lentils, with a topping of deeply caramelised dry-fried onions, koushari is always served with sauces on the side. Street-food vendors, pushing mobile handcarts laden with bowls of pasta and rice, sell this popular, cheap and filling dish. It's also to be found in many eateries, especially in Cairo.

Ibrahim Rashed, executive chef onboard *Sun Boat IV*, makes a batch of kousheri especially for me. His epicurean version contains the addition of chickpeas, two types of pasta and several spices, along with the obligatory lentils, rice and fried onions. Two sauces accompany his creation – a fresh tomato sauce and a hot chilli salsa. I would not have thought to combine so many grains and starches in one tasty dish. It is a revelation.

BAKED KIBBEH kibbeh bi-sayniyeh

Kibbeh may be served raw (see *kibbeh naiyeh*, page 61) or cooked in different forms. This slab of kibbeh baked in a tray is a homely and very comforting rendition of this, the national dish of Lebanon. Sliced, it can be eaten hot or cold, with perhaps a salad on the side – I recommend Oriental salad (see page 34) as a refreshing accompaniment.

I cup fine burghul

500g fresh lean boneless lamb
from the leg, trimmed of skin & fat

I medium onion, finely chopped

2 tablespoons cold water

¼ teaspoon ground allspice

¼ teaspoon ground cinnamon

I teaspoon sea salt

¼ teaspoon ground black pepper

2 tablespoons pine nuts or walnuts

3 tablespoons olive oil

serves 6

1 Preheat oven to 175°C. Lightly oil a 20cm square baking dish or a 22cm round baking dish. Place burghul in a bowl and cover with boiling water. Leave to soften for 15 minutes, then drain well. Rinse with cold water to cool burghul, then squeeze out as much water as possible.

2 Finely dice lamb, then mince in a food processor. Add burghul, onion, water, spices, salt and pepper to lamb in food processor and process in short bursts until amalgamated but not too mushy.

3 Pat meat mixture into prepared pan. Cut into 5cm square or diamond shapes, arrange a pine nut or walnut in the centre of each and drizzle with olive oil. Bake for 30–35 minutes, or until firm and lightly browned. Serve kibbeh from the pan or invert onto a serving platter.

4 Alternatively, make a simplified version of kibbeh. With damp hands, mould the mixture into oval or round patties and pan-fry to brown on both sides.

KIBBEH NAIYEH

Kibbeh naiyeh is a traditional Lebanese dish of raw minced lamb bound into patties with burghul wheat. This is like a Middle Eastern alternative to steak tartare. If raw lamb does not appeal, there is a version of cooked lamb kibbeh on page 60 and an interesting vegetable version of these rissoles as well on page 63.

As with so many traditional recipes, notions of what makes good kibbeh taste great will vary from family to family. Some cooks like to add finely chopped parsley and mint, while others prefer their kibbeh plain so that the pure tastes of lamb and burghal are highlighted. This recipe is for simple kibbeh, to which you can add herbs, if you wish. Whichever version you recreate, raw kibbeh is incredibly rich, so only dainty servings are needed to fully appreciate this dish.

½ cup fine burghul

300g fresh lean boneless lamb from the leg, trimmed of skin & fat

½ small onion, very finely diced

½ teaspoon sea salt

½ teaspoon ground allspice

bowl of cold water with added ice cubes

garnish options

radishes

spring onions

red peppers

pickled vegetables

serves 6

1 Place burghul in a bowl and cover with boiling water. Leave to soften for 15 minutes, then drain well. Rinse with cold water to cool burghul, then squeeze out as much water as possible.

2 Finely dice lamb, then grind in a food processor, using short bursts so the lamb does not become too warm or too mushy.

3 Transfer mixture to a bowl and mix in chopped onion, salt and allspice. Knead burghul into lamb mixture, dipping hands in iced water as needed for smoothness.

4 Mould finished mix into a dome on a plate, garnish with sprigs of parsley and serve with flatbread, radishes, spring onions, red peppers or pickled vegetables on the side.

POTATO KIBBEH

We came across several versions of this ancient vegetarian kibbeh recipe. This is one made with potatoes that I particularly enjoyed.

filling

3 tablespoons olive oil

2 onions, finely diced

1 clove garlic, crushed

¼ teaspoon allspice

5 tablespoons pine nuts

4 tablespoons currants

3 tablespoons tahini

sea salt & freshly ground black pepper

potato mixture

6 medium floury potatoes,
peeled & quartered

1½ cups fine burghul

sea salt & freshly ground black pepper

½ cup flour to coat

1–2 litres sunflower or light olive oil
for deep-frying

makes 24

1 Heat a frying pan, add oil, onions and garlic and cook over a medium heat for 10 minutes or until softened but lightly browned. Stir in remaining ingredients and season with salt and pepper to taste.

Potato mixture

1 Cook potatoes in boiling salted water until tender. Drain well and mash. At the same time, place burghul wheat in a bowl and cover with boiling water. Leave to stand for 15 minutes to soften. Drain softened burghul and add to mashed potatoes. Season with salt and pepper and mix well to combine into a paste.

2 Take a heaped tablespoonful of this mixture and with wet hands flatten it into a disc. Place a teaspoonful of filling into the centre of the disc, then mould potato paste around filling to form an oval ball. Repeat process until all the mixture is formed into stuffed oval-shaped balls. Place these on a tray and chill for 30 minutes.

3 Heat oil in a heavy-based saucepan. Test temperature of the oil for frying by dropping in a crust of bread – it should bubble, rise to the surface and turn golden brown. Place flour on a tray and roll formed balls in flour to coat lightly.

4 Drop batches of stuffed balls into hot oil and cook for 3–4 minutes or until golden brown. Drain on paper towels and serve while hot.

FALAFEL

Although most closely associated with Israel, falafel are made all over the Middle East. Eaten as a snack food or sandwiched into pockets of pita bread, falafel make a sustaining meal. These same rissoles are called *ta'miyah* in Cairo, where they are made with broad beans and are claimed as one of the national dishes of Egypt. In Lebanon, Syria and Jordan falafel are more commonly made with chickpeas, or a mixture of the two. Large, skinned, dried and split broad beans are the authentic ones to use but can be hard to find outside the Middle East, so here I've given a recipe using only chickpeas, as these are more commonly available.

64

1 cup dried chickpeas, soaked overnight in plenty of cold water

2 tablespoons olive oil

1 onion, chopped

4 cloves garlic, crushed

1 teaspoon each ground coriander & cumin

pinch cayenne pepper

½ cup chopped fresh parsley

½ cup chopped fresh coriander

1 teaspoon baking powder

sea salt & freshly ground black pepper

1 litre sunflower or light olive oil for frying

serves 4

1 Drain chickpeas and discard soaking liquid. Place chickpeas in a large saucepan and cover with plenty of fresh cold water. Bring to the boil, then turn down heat, cover and simmer gently for 1 hour or until very tender. Drain chickpeas well and set aside to cool.

2 At the same time, heat a saucepan, add oil and onion and cook onion over a medium heat for 5 minutes to soften but not colour. Add garlic and spices and fry for 1 minute longer. Remove to cool.

3 Grind drained chickpeas in a food processor to resemble fine breadcrumbs. Add cooled onion mixture and remaining ingredients and process to form a smooth, soft paste that will hold together into balls. If necessary, it is possible to add an egg or 2 tablespoons of flour to bind the mixture. Set mixture aside to rest for 30 minutes.

4 With slightly damp hands, mould mixture into ovals, round balls or flat patties, as preferred.

5 Heat oil in a heavy-based saucepan. Test temperature of the oil for frying by dropping in a crust of bread — it should bubble, rise to the surface and turn golden brown. Fry falafel in batches until golden brown all over. Remove with a slotted spoon to drain on paper towels.

MELTING CHICKPEAS

I had dinner one evening in Beirut with Houda Bouri (Greg Malouf's charming aunt). Houda took me to a fabulous restaurant where a dish like this one was served. The chickpeas were so meltingly tender and delicious – I couldn't get the dish out of my mind. As soon as I returned home I was determined to recreate the memorable chickpea recipe – and this is the result.

1 cup dried chickpeas, soaked
overnight in plenty of cold water
¼ cup olive oil
1 large onion, finely chopped
4 cloves garlic, chopped
1 teaspoon ground cumin
sea salt & freshly ground black pepper
extra virgin olive oil

serves 6

1 Drain chickpeas and discard soaking liquid. Place chickpeas in a large saucepan and cover with plenty of fresh cold water. Bring to the boil, then turn down heat, cover and simmer gently for 1 hour or until very tender. Drain well.

2 Heat a frying pan, add ¼ cup measured olive oil and the onion and cook over a medium heat for 10 minutes until onion is softened but not coloured. Add garlic and cumin and cook for 1 minute longer to release flavours.

3 Add drained chickpeas and 1 cup of cooking liquid. Simmer for 15 minutes, stirring frequently until chickpeas melt into the onion mixture. Season with salt and pepper to taste. Remove to a bowl to cool to room temperature. Serve drizzled with extra virgin olive oil.

KOUSHERI

Today, this very old Egyptian dish is an extremely popular staple meal. Street-food vendors serve bowls of *housheri* from carts or holes-in-the-wall and many Cairo restaurants sell kousheri to eat in or take out. Kousheri, meaning 'messy mix', is traditionally served with two sauces, one tomato and one spicy, and more often than not topped with fried or pickled red onions.

Ibrahim Rashed, executive chef onboard Abercrombie and Kent's *Sun Boat IV* kindly demonstrated many local dishes to me as we cruised the Nile. Kousheri was one such revelation. I was delighted to be offered his version of this authentic recipe.

½ cup dried chickpeas, soaked overnight in plenty of cold water

½ cup brown lentils, soaked overnight in plenty of cold water

½ cup short grain rice, rinsed in running cold water

½ cup broken vermicelli pasta

1 cup small pasta shapes, such as macaroni

2–3 tablespoons olive oil

2 large onions, finely sliced & deep-fried as a garnish

3 cloves garlic

½ teaspoon each ground coriander & cumin

pinch chilli powder

sea salt & freshly ground black pepper

tomato sauce & spicy chilli sauce to serve (recipes follow)

serves 4

1 Drain chickpeas and discard soaking liquid. Place chickpeas in a large saucepan and cover with plenty of fresh cold water. Bring to the boil, then turn down heat, cover and simmer gently for 1 hour or until tender. Drain well. In another saucepan, cook brown lentils in plenty of water for 30–40 minutes or until tender, then drain well.

2 In separate saucepans, cook rice in boiling water for 12 minutes or until tender to the bite, then drain well. Cook pastas in boiling salted water for 7–10 minutes or according to packet instructions until tender to the bite, then drain well.

3 Heat a frying pan, add oil and onions and cook over a medium high heat for 8–10 minutes, stirring frequently until onions are browned and crisp. Remove to one side – these onions are a garnish.

4 Add garlic and spices to remaining oil in the pan and cook gently for 1 minute, stirring constantly, to release flavours. Add cooked chickpeas, pastas, rice and lentils, and stir and toss to coat in the flavoured oil and to heat through. Season with salt and pepper to taste.

5 Serve kousheri garnished with browned onions and with tomato and chilli sauces on the side.

tomato sauce for kousheri

3 tablespoons vegetable or olive oil
2 cloves garlic, chopped
1 teaspoon ground coriander
pinch chilli powder
1 tablespoon soft brown sugar
¼ cup red wine vinegar
400g can tomatoes, coarsely chopped
sea salt & freshly ground black pepper

makes 1 cup

1 Heat a saucepan, add oil, garlic and spices and cook for 1 minute, stirring constantly. Add sugar, vinegar and tomatoes and bring to the boil.

2 Turn down the heat and simmer gently for 20 minutes or until thick. Season with salt and pepper to taste.

chilli sauce for kousheri

4 red chillies, seeds removed, flesh chopped
1 tablespoon tomato paste
1 tablespoon sugar
1 teaspoon salt
¼ cup red wine vinegar
½ cup water

makes ½ cup

1 Place all ingredients in a saucepan and bring to the boil. Simmer for 5 minutes or until reduced by half. Remove to cool.

TOASTED RICE PILAF *pilaf mahammer*

This simple side dish of nutty flavoured rice, known as *pilaf mahammer*, could not be easier to prepare, nor more delicious. Serve it as an accompaniment to any of the stew-like dishes in this book.

100g butter
2 cups basmati rice
sea salt

serves 6

1   Melt butter in a large saucepan. Add half the rice and toast gently over a medium heat for about 5 minutes or until it becomes translucent.

2   Add remaining rice and cover with hot water. Bring to the boil, then turn down heat to gently simmer for 20 minutes. Drain off any excess liquid and season rice with salt to taste.

3   Half the rice will be white and half chestnut brown, creating an attractive side dish.

69

JEWELLED RICE

Resembling a rich golden tapestry studded with ruby-red seeds and other colourful jewels, this rice dish holds a magical wealth of flavours. Originating in Persia, jewelled rice dishes can today be found in other parts of the Middle East, where the combinations of fruits and nuts may vary.

2 good pinches saffron threads

¼ cup boiling water

2 cups basmati rice

2 tablespoons olive oil

1 tablespoon butter

¾ cup barberries, or substitute dried cranberries

½ cup currants

½ cup dried apricots, finely sliced

zest of 2 oranges

¼ cup slivered almonds

¼ cup slivered pistachio nuts

sea salt

serves 6–8

1 Place saffron threads in a small bowl with measured boiling water and leave to soak for 10 minutes. Soak rice in plenty of cold water for 10 minutes, then rinse under running cold water until the water runs clear, draining well.

2 Bring a saucepan full of water to the boil, add rice, simmer steadily for 10 minutes, then drain well.

3 Heat a large, heavy-based saucepan. Add oil and butter to melt. Add drained, hot rice, then stir in saffron and soaking liquid. Stir in all remaining ingredients and season with salt to taste.

4 Cover pan tightly and leave over a very low heat for 5–8 minutes to steam heat through and finish cooking rice. Fluff up rice and serve.

LEBANESE GIANT COUSCOUS WITH CHICKEN moghrabieh

Moghrabieh, meaning 'North African', is a large-grain couscous made with semolina like the North African version that obviously inspired this ingredient. These giant balls of couscous, which is essentially a semolina pasta, need to be soaked before cooking. Moghrabieh is most often cooked with whole chicken to form a rustic, thick type of chicken soup, but I have modernised this concept slightly by using chicken breasts in my recipe. I don't know if Lebanese moghrabieh is available globally, however, I have come across other versions of giant couscous, such as Israeli couscous and Sardinian *fregola*, that could easily be substituted in this recipe.

72

2 tablespoons olive oil

1 onion, finely diced

1½ cups giant couscous (moghrabieh)

4 cups chicken stock

3 skinless chicken breasts, trimmed of fat

15g butter

sea salt & freshly ground black pepper

zest & juice of 2 lemons

¼ cup chopped fresh coriander

¼ cup chopped fresh parsley

2 tablespoons chopped fresh mint

serves 6

1 Heat a large saucepan, add olive oil and onion and cook over a moderate heat for 5–10 minutes until onion is softened but not coloured. At the same time place giant couscous in a saucepan of boiling water and simmer for 5 minutes, then drain well.

2 Stir couscous in with the onions, add stock and bring to the boil, then turn down the heat and simmer for 10 minutes, stirring regularly.

3 Slice chicken breasts and add to the pan. Add more stock to moisten if necessary and simmer for 5 minutes more until grains of couscous are tender to the bite and most of the liquid has been absorbed.

4 Stir through butter to add richness, and season with salt and pepper to taste. Stir through lemon zest and juice and chopped herbs.

pyramids
of nuts &
seeds

nuts & seeds

Pyramids of nuts and seeds, piled high on open tins or bursting from coarse sacks, are static displays in the souk. There are almonds, walnuts, hazelnuts, highly prized pistachio nuts, sesame and poppy seeds, and pine nuts a plenty. Vendors scoop handfuls into bags or wrap small select amounts in Arabic script newsprint to be carried off as a snack. This is a lively, social scene where people converse enthusiastically and always taste before they buy.

Typically, the souk is not just a food market but the social heartbeat of a community. People come to buy foodstuffs and ingredients, of course, but also to meet, talk and catch up with friends. My friend Asma tells me that visiting the souk is a very convivial time. 'We shop, we exchange news, we drink coffee, and discuss what's new in the market,' she explains.

Nuts are widely used in Middle Eastern cooking, and often in unexpected ways, such as using ground nuts to thicken and add texture to sauces and stews. Consider Circassian chicken, which features an intriguing and delicious sauce based on ground walnuts. And also *muhammara*, a vibrant mezze dip of walnuts pounded with red peppers found in Syria, Lebanon, Jordan and Turkey.

Tahini, a paste made of ground sesame seeds, is used as an ingredient to add flavour to many classic dips and sauces. Or it may form the basis of a sauce itself, as in sesame *taratour*. Taratour is a wonderfully rich-flavoured sauce, which can alternatively be made with pine nuts, and in Turkey is made with walnuts. The process of making your own taratour is easy and incredibly satisfying, and this savoury sauce is the perfect tasty complement to baked fish, skewered meats or vegetable dishes.

The addition of nuts to stews to enhance the flavour and add textural contrast is a culinary tradition dating from the time of the Persian Empire, when nuts indicated opulence. Persian nut-based sauces are classic, such as *fesenjân*, a crushed walnut and tart pomegranate molasses sauce that is served with duck or chicken, and sometimes fish or vegetables.

Many salads, savoury pies, breads, conserves, pickles, rice dishes and stuffed vegetables incorporate nuts and seeds. Pine nuts, especially, turn up in every kind of dish. Bowls of nuts, blanched or toasted, are often served to greet visitors, or may be included with fruits to finish a meal.

Sweet-shop vendors offer richly layered and sugar-drenched pastries that include pulverised nuts, such as the much-loved baklava, which is popularly eaten at celebrations and festivals. My all-time favourite is the walnut-stuffed ma'amoul, or perhaps the pistachio-filled birds' nests made with shredded pastry, or ... well, it's hard to say, as there are literally hundreds of varieties and they're all very pleasing.

Throughout the Middle East, nuts can also be found in cakes (based on ground nuts instead of flour) and desserts, or ground into a marzipan-like paste and stuffed into dates or figs. Almonds, pistachios or hazelnuts can be found embedded in nougat and Turkish delight. There's also sesame halva, a sweetmeat made of ground sesame seeds and honey or sugar, which is sold in slices taken from huge slabs. A type of fairy floss, *pashmak* is a sugary speciality from Iran, made from ground sesame seeds and sugar, which is spun into candy floss.

Nuts and seeds play a part too in much of the simple, rustic food that is offered from street stalls found all over the Middle East, from Iran and Turkey to the Gulf States and the Eastern Mediterranean crescent. The atmosphere of the surroundings and the engaging vendors are often as stimulating as the tastes themselves. The seller of kebabs stands in front of a charcoal fire while smoky vapours spurt from the meat to sharpen the appetite. The barbecued meat is served with a sauce of ground pine nuts.

It is still wintry when we visit Turkey and Azerbaijan so we are able to enjoy the warming experience of eating roasted chestnuts, bought piping hot from a street vendor and nibbled as we wander and explore. Almonds and pistachios are served grilled and salted. And in Egypt, dukkah, a melange of hazelnuts ground with spices and seeds, is dispensed in paper cones and eaten as a dip with bread and olive oil.

CIRCASSIAN CHICKEN

Circassian slaves brought this recipe to their Ottoman rulers. It is now enjoyed as a buffet dish or sometimes as part of a mezze table. I recommend preparing this chicken dish a couple of days in advance. Stored covered in the fridge, the flavours meld together, improving with time.

1.5kg chicken, washed & patted
dry with paper towels

2 small onions, sliced

2 cloves garlic, chopped

good pinch saffron threads

sea salt & freshly ground black pepper

3 slices white bread, crusts removed

2 cups fresh walnut pieces

I teaspoon paprika

¼ teaspoon cayenne pepper

¼ teaspoon ground allspice

juice of I lemon

fresh parsley to serve

paprika oil

2 tablespoons walnut oil

I teaspoon paprika

¼ teaspoon cayenne pepper

serves 6

1 Season chicken with salt and pepper and place in a large saucepan with onions, garlic and saffron. Cover with cold water and bring to the boil, then turn down heat and simmer gently for I½ hours, until chicken is cooked. Do not boil as this will make the chicken tough.

2 Remove chicken to one side, leaving cooking liquid in saucepan. Remove skin and bones from chicken. Add bones to cooking liquid in saucepan and boil liquid until reduced by half. Strain this stock and skim off any fat from surface.

3 Meanwhile, cut chicken flesh into pieces and place in a bowl. Cover and refrigerate until cold. Place bread in a bowl with ¼ cup stock and leave to soften.

4 Place walnuts, spices and wet bread in the bowl of a food processor and grind to a paste. Slowly add I cup of hot stock and process — adding more stock if necessary to make a smooth creamy sauce. Season with salt and pepper to taste and set aside to cool.

5 Combine walnut sauce and lemon juice. Arrange chicken on a serving plate and coat with sauce. Cover and refrigerate for I–2 days before serving. Serve drizzled with paprika oil (made simply by combining walnut oil and spices) and scatter with parsley.

FISH HARRA-STYLE

This very hot and spicy sauce originates from the Northern Lebanese town of Tripoli, famed for its fish dishes. However, we did eat renditions of this dish in other countries, such as Jordan and the Gulf States. Sometimes the costly walnuts were omitted from the sauce, giving a different but acceptable result. Alternatively, *harra* sauce can be served as a mezze dish with pita bread to dip.

3 tablespoons olive oil

3 cloves garlic, coarsely chopped

1½ cups fresh walnut pieces, finely chopped

½ teaspoon ground cinnamon

1 teaspoon ground coriander

¼ teaspoon cayenne pepper or chilli powder

1 red chilli, seeds removed, flesh chopped

juice of 2 lemons

2 large tomatoes, peeled & coarsely chopped

½ cup tightly packed fresh coriander leaves

½ cup tightly packed fresh parsley leaves

sea salt & freshly ground black pepper

1.5kg whole fish, cleaned, scaled & rinsed (I use red snapper)

10 preserved vine leaves

serves 4

1 Heat a frying pan, add oil and garlic and cook over a medium heat for a few seconds before adding walnuts, dry spices and chilli to fry gently for a few minutes, stirring continuously.

2 Add lemon juice, tomatoes and herbs and simmer gently for 2 minutes. Add a little water if necessary to bring the mixture to a sauce consistency. Season with salt and pepper to taste and set aside to cool.

3 Preheat oven to 180°C. Rinse fish and pat dry with paper towels. Slash 3 diagonal cuts on each side of the fish and season inside and out with salt and pepper. Place fish in a lightly oiled oven pan lined with vine leaves. Vine leaves are not traditional here but I find they add to the attractive presentation of this dish, plus they are an excellent way to line the cooking pan.

4 Pack half the sauce inside the fish and spoon remaining sauce over the fish. Bake for 35–40 minutes, or until fish tests cooked.

TAHINI SAUCE OR DIP tahini taratour

I once catered for a Lebanese wedding and this tahini sauce, served in the traditional way with baked fish, was the family's special request. To make a whiter tahini sauce, blend the water with the tahini first, then add the lemon juice. *Tahini taratour* can be thinned with water or lemon juice, depending on how you want to use the sauce. It makes a lovely thick dip to serve as mezze. Thinned, it can be used as a salad dressing or to drizzle over falafel sandwiches, for example.

1 clove garlic, crushed

1 teaspoon sea salt

½ cup tahini

½ cup water

¼ cup lemon juice, to taste

makes 1 cup

1 Combine garlic, salt and tahini in a bowl. Gradually blend in water and then lemon juice – the mixture will first thicken and then dilute to a smooth sauce. For a thicker sauce, add less water. You may need to add a little more lemon juice, to taste.

2 To make tahini sauce with parsley, add ¼ cup chopped fresh parsley. This makes a delicious dip, or a sauce to coat baked or poached fish or chicken. Store refrigerated in a sealed jar.

PINE NUT SAUCE pine nut taratour

This nutty garlic sauce is popular in Lebanon, Syria, Egypt and Turkey where it is commonly used as a sauce for fish or seafood, though it can also be served as a dip.

1 slice white bread, soaked in ¼ cup cold water to soften

1 cup pine nuts (or walnuts can be substituted, if preferred)

5 cloves garlic

½ teaspoon sea salt

½ cup lemon juice

¼ cup olive oil

parsley leaves to garnish

paprika or cayenne pepper to garnish

makes 1½ cups

1 Combine all ingredients, except garnish, in the bowl of a food processor and blend to form a smooth paste the consistency of thick yoghurt.

2 Like tahini taratour (above), this pine nut taratour can be served as a sauce for fish or as a dip for pita bread or fresh vegetables. Serve garnished with parsley and paprika or cayenne.

SESAME SEED CANDY

All kinds of sweetmeats are highly favoured throughout the Middle East. This example is a seed toffee simply made from honey and sesame seeds.

olive oil to grease tray

3 cups honey

2 cups sesame seeds

makes 25

1 Lightly grease a baking tray with oil. Place honey in a large heavy-based saucepan and simmer over a low heat, stirring regularly to prevent boiling over, until it reaches the hard-crack stage — this will take up to 45 minutes. Test by dropping a spoonful into cold water — mixture should form a small hard ball.

2 Take great care not to burn yourself on the hot toffee-like mixture. Stir in the sesame seeds. Pour the candy mixture onto prepared baking tray and set tray on a cooling rack.

3 When cooled but not hard, score diamond shapes into candy. When completely cold, remove candy from tray and cut to fully separate pieces.

NUT & POMEGRANATE SEED SYRUP

Like a plateful of glittering jewels, this combination of ruby-red pomegranate seeds and mixed nuts is a complete delight to view. The pretty combination is also a taste sensation. As pomegranates are a symbol of love and fertility, this dish is often served at celebrations, such as engagement parties. I like to use it as a topping for *muhallabiah* (see photograph, page 128).

¼ cup blanched almonds

¼ cup slivered pistachio nuts

¼ cup pine nuts

3 pomegranates

1 recipe floral sugar syrup (see page 162)

serves 4

1 Place all nuts in a bowl and cover with cold water. Leave to soak for 1 hour, then drain well.

2 Halve pomegranates and remove seeds; discard pith and skin. Combine pomegranate seeds with nuts.

3 Make floral sugar according to the recipe and, while still warm, pour this over the seeds and nuts. Stir to combine, then chill well to serve.

DAMASCENE SHORTBREAD WITH PISTACHIO NUTS *ghoraibah*

Although this particular recipe hails from Damascus, each Middle Eastern country has its own version of these shortbread biscuits. They are wonderfully short and sweet and just the thing to enjoy with a small glass of strong Arabic coffee or tea.

150g butter, softened
1¼ cups icing sugar
2 cups flour, sifted
20 blanched pistachio nuts

makes 20

82

1 Place butter and icing sugar in a bowl and beat with an electric mixer until pale and creamy. Mix in flour, turn out onto a work surface and knead lightly to bring together and form a smooth dough. Wrap dough in plastic wrap and refrigerate to rest for 1 hour.

2 Preheat oven to 180°C. Line a baking tray with non-stick baking paper. Divide dough into 20 equal portions. Roll each portion into a ball and place on prepared baking tray. Press to flatten, then press a pistachio nut into the centre of each biscuit. Repeat this process with remaining portions.

3 Bake shortbread for 15–20 minutes or until pale golden. Remove to a wire rack to cool. Store in an airtight container.

The *Imam* (Muslim holy man) was said to have fainted when he first tasted an exquisite dish of stuffed eggplants cooked in a copious amount of good olive oil. Legend has it that he fainted with shock when he saw how much expensive olive oil was used in the making of this dish. Another version of the story says he swooned with pleasure because the dish was so delicious. I like the second version best, as this shows how resourceful Middle Eastern cooks have the ability to transform everyday vegetables into something extraordinary.

While Middle Eastern dishes are often simple and rustic, the flavours are bold because cooks work with the seasons and choose ingredients well. Local seasonal produce has intense flavour and colour – deep purple eggplants, plump heritage tomatoes, delicate cucumbers, pale sweet courgettes, blushing radishes, crisp lettuces and fat orange pumpkins – and this bounty is concentrated by imaginative cooking.

The large central market in Baku, Azerbaijan, is full of surprises. There is a bleak isolation here, though perhaps the grey weather does not help. This is far from a Mediterranean-style climate and I do not expect such profusion and availability of produce. There are marvellous displays of everything from giant pumpkins and bittersweet pomegranates to black market caviar and whole sturgeon fish; and a plethora of products in between. A farmer holds a live turkey in his arms; eager vendors display curiously large flatbreads; and jars of colourful pickles are lined up in rows.

Here, too, are interesting dried vegetables – eggplants, marrows and peppers – strung up as garlands. These dried vegetables are common in Middle Eastern cuisines and are easily reconstituted in water. Drying is just one way vegetables are preserved for use later in the year when the fresh produce is not in season.

After our market experience we are welcomed into the home of our friend, Zauer Aliyev, who lives with his extended family in a small complex of homes in the outer suburbs of Azerbaijan's capital city, Baku. Zauer's sister, Chimna, and cousin-in-law, Savinj, have invited us for a day of traditional cooking. Historically, the cuisine of Azerbaijan developed close to Persian and Turkish food and much similarity can be seen between these national cuisines.

Resplendent in frilly aprons, we set to work on a faded, well-scrubbed tabletop, making dishes as they have been made in this same kitchen for generations. We make *dushpara*, a broth of

extremely tiny, hand-formed ravioli-like dumplings; stuffed vegetables; and vegetable fillings for a thin bread known as *kutap*. This food is healthy and honest, and the women show me that cooking these age-old dishes involves elements of intuition, skill and routine.

Rolling out the dough for kutap takes much practice. Savinj rolls and spins and flicks a circle of dough around with a very fine rolling pin, narrower than the width of a broom handle, until the disc of dough is almost paper-thin. She has a light touch and this process appears effortless, until I attempt to do the same. It is not as easy as Savinj makes it look. But after a slightly awkward start, repetition does help establish a rhythm and increase my ability. The breads are filled with mashed pumpkin or a mixture of spinach and herbs, then browned in a dry skillet to produce a mouth-watering snack.

Throughout the Middle East, foods that are stuffed, such as vegetables or vine leaves, are known as *dolma*, *dolmeh*, *dolmathes*, *mahshi* and various other forms of the same word. All the lands touched by the Ottoman Empire have embraced the practice of stuffing vegetables. While some versions are stuffed with rice, today Chimna and Savinj fill peppers, tomatoes and onions with a mixture of minced lamb.

There is no stove in the kitchen so all the cooking is done over a single gas ring. Chimna heats olive oil in a deep pot until it pops expectantly, before spreading a layer of onion and lamb to brown. We remove the insides from the vegetables and refill them with the lamb mixture. The tomato pulp is used to make a light fragrant sauce for the vegetables and everything is returned to the pot. Set over the low flame, the stuffed vegetables cook slowly until blissfully tender and succulent.

After a long and companionable day in the kitchen, we all gather around the table to share the fruits of our labours.

the Imam fainted

OKRA IN TOMATO SAUCE

Courgettes or beans are also delicious cooked in this same manner – simply substitute an equal weight of beans or thickly sliced courgettes for the okra and cut the cooking time a little. This dish of okra, or ladies' fingers as they are also called, is often made with the addition of meat, similar to a meat and okra stew.

400g okra

olive oil

1 onion, finely sliced

4 cloves garlic, chopped

1 green chilli, seeds removed, flesh finely chopped

¼ cup coarsely chopped fresh coriander

400g can tomatoes, coarsely chopped

sea salt & freshly ground black pepper

serves 4

1 Neatly trim or peel off stem end of okra to form points. Wash okra in cold water to thoroughly remove any grit. Drain in a colander, then pat dry with paper towels.

2 Heat a large non-stick frying pan, add 4 tablespoons olive oil and fry okra in 2–3 batches, tossing for 2–3 minutes over a medium heat until crisp but not browned. This will seal the okra and prevent it from releasing a disconcerting glutinous substance, which is a characteristic secretion of okra. This particular dish is nicer without the addition of this natural thickening agent. Remove okra to drain on paper towels.

3 Add onion to the pan and cook for 5–10 minutes, stirring frequently until golden brown. Add garlic, chilli and coriander and cook for 1 minute more. Pour in canned tomatoes and bring to the boil.

4 Now add okra, turn down the heat and simmer gently for 20 minutes until the tomato sauce is thick. Season with salt and pepper to taste.

(see photograph, page 84, rear)

ARTICHOKES STUFFED WITH PARSLEY & BROAD BEANS

This is an incredibly pretty combination full of delightful flavours. Frozen broad beans are excellent to use instead of fresh, if the need arises. Run these under hot water to thaw — they need no further cooking.

8 large preserved artichoke bottoms

500g broad beans, pods & outer shells removed to reveal the bright green beans

½ cup fresh flat-leaf parsley leaves

100g feta cheese, crumbled

2 cloves garlic, crushed

1 tablespoon lemon juice

3 tablespoons extra virgin olive oil

sea salt & freshly ground black pepper

serves 6

1 Place artichoke bottoms on a serving platter. Combine broad beans, parsley leaves and feta in a bowl.

2 Make a dressing by whisking together garlic with lemon juice and olive oil. Season with salt and pepper to taste. Pour dressing over broad bean salad mixture and toss well. Spoon a little salad into each artichoke bottom. Serve at room temperature.

Note: If you can't find preserved artichoke bottoms, substitute artichoke hearts in this recipe. These will be too small to stuff, but you can simply toss all the ingredients together and serve as a salad dish.

(see photograph, page 84, front)

SWEET & SOUR PUMPKIN & LAMB STEW

This is one of the many types of stews that are common in Iran and Northern Syria. These stews are modestly spiced but flavoured with sour juices to give a typical sweet-sour taste. Serve with fluffy steamed rice for a rich and satisfying meal.

88

¾ cup dried chickpeas, soaked overnight in plenty of cold water

3 tablespoons olive oil

500g lamb shoulder steaks, trimmed of fat & cut into 3cm cubes

1 onion, finely sliced

2 teaspoons ground cumin

1 teaspoon paprika

1 teaspoon ground allspice

1 cinnamon stick

400g can chopped tomatoes

1½ cups beef stock

500g pumpkin, peel & seeds removed, flesh coarsely sliced

juice of 1 lemon or 1 tablespoon pomegranate molasses

sea salt & freshly ground black pepper

¼ cup chopped fresh coriander

serves 4

1 Drain chickpeas and discard soaking liquid. Place chickpeas in a large saucepan and cover with plenty of fresh cold water. Bring to the boil, then turn down heat, cover and simmer gently for 1 hour or until very tender. Drain well.

2 Heat oil in a large saucepan and brown lamb in 2–3 batches. Remove to one side. Add onion to the pan and cook over a medium heat for 5 minutes. Add spices and stir-fry for 1 minute.

3 Add tomatoes and stock and boil for 5 minutes, stirring to scrape up any flavour residue from the base of the pan. Return lamb to the pan, then turn down the heat and simmer gently for 1 hour.

4 Stir in pumpkin and drained chickpeas. Cover pan and simmer gently for 30 minutes more until meat is tender. Season with lemon juice or pomegranate molasses and salt and pepper to taste. Serve scattered with fresh coriander.

RED PEPPER SALAD
WITH POMEGRANATE MOLASSES DRESSING

Pomegranate molasses dressing gives a contrasting tartness to the sweetness of the roast red peppers. This interplay of sweet and sour flavours is a typical Middle Eastern combination.

5 red peppers
olive oil
2–3 tablespoons torn fresh mint leaves
to garnish

serves 6

1 Preheat oven to 200°C. Halve the red peppers and remove core, seeds and white membrane. Place pepper halves in an oven pan, cut-side down, and rub with a little olive oil. Bake for 30 minutes or until skins blister.

2 Transfer to a bowl, cover and stand 10 minutes to sweat, then peel off the skins (they will slip off easily). Cut each pepper half into 2 or 3 strips, toss with pomegranate molasses dressing. Arrange in a serving dish and garnish with mint leaves.

pomegranate molasses dressing
1 tablespoon pomegranate molasses
3 tablespoons extra virgin olive oil
sea salt & freshly ground black pepper

makes ¼ cup

1 Place pomegranate molasses and olive oil in a bowl and whisk to combine. Season with salt and pepper to taste.

(see photograph, page 90)

GREEN BEAN SALAD

This is a simple bean salad made special with a topping of lemony onions. Soaking red onions in lemon juice (or sometimes vinegar) softens the onions, changing their taste and texture significantly. Some people like to sprinkle the finished dish with sumac to heighten the lemony flavour.

500g fine green beans, trimmed & halved
¼ cup fresh flat-leaf parsley leaves to garnish

serves 4

1   Cook beans in boiling salted water for 3–4 minutes or until they are just tender but still retain their green colour. Drain well, refresh in ice-cold water to cool. Drain and arrange on a serving platter. Scatter with lemony onions and parsley.

lemony onions
2 small red onions, finely sliced
juice of 2 lemons
sea salt

makes 1 cup

1   Place sliced onions and lemon juice in a ceramic bowl. Sprinkle with a little salt and set aside to soak for 4 hours, or overnight.

2   Drain and discard soaking liquid. Serve onions as a type of garnish or as a salad component.

SPINACH WITH RAISINS & PINE NUTS

We stopped one day to take photos of groups of Syrian women picking spinach from a field. This was a memorable interlude. The women shyly posed for photos, their eyes shining out from under broad-brimmed sun hats, worn to protect them from the hot sun. We seemed to chat without language in common and I feel they seemed as pleased to pass the time of day with us as we were with them. This recipe cooks spinach in olive oil (a common practice), the spinach is then topped with Moorish flavours of raisins and pine nuts. This makes a good mezze or side dish.

¼ cup olive oil
3 onions, finely sliced
1 teaspoon ground coriander
500g washed spinach, stems removed
juice of 1 lemon
sea salt & freshly ground black pepper
¼ cup raisins
¼ cup toasted pine nuts

serves 6

1   Heat a non-stick frying pan, add oil and onions and cook over a medium heat for 10 minutes or until onions are a deep golden brown. Remove ½ cup of this mixture and keep for the garnish.

2   Add ground coriander to the pan and cook for 1 minute. Coarsely slice spinach and add to pan — cook over a medium heat for 5–10 minutes, tossing frequently as spinach wilts and liquid evaporates. Stir in lemon juice and season with salt and pepper.

3   Serve warm garnished with reserved onions and scattered with raisins and toasted pine nuts.

STUFFED PEPPERS, TOMATOES & COURGETTES

All the lands that have been touched by the Ottoman Empire have embraced the practice of stuffing vegetables in this way, known as dolma or dolmeh. I spent a remarkable day in a simple Azebaijani kitchen with Chimna and Sevinj showing me the secrets of their cuisine. They made stuffed vegetables filled with lamb, but I also enjoy the version stuffed with rice, so I have given both recipes here.

4 large tomatoes
2 red peppers
4 medium courgettes

1   Slice tops off tomatoes and reserve. Scoop out pulp with a spoon and reserve. Turn tomatoes cut-side down on paper towels to drain.

2   Slice peppers in half and remove seeds and white membranes. Halve courgettes lengthways. Scoop out central seed canal with a teaspoon, and discard.

3   Preheat oven to 180°C. Fill tomatoes and pepper halves with either rice or meat mixture, as preferred (recipes follow). Replace tomato tops. Place vegetables in an oven pan and drizzle with olive oil.

4   Finely chop reserved tomato pulp and spoon this around the vegetables. Add white wine or water to the pan and a little salt and pepper – this will form a light tomato sauce for the vegetables. Bake, uncovered, for 30 minutes.

rice filling

olive oil
1 onion, chopped
2 cloves garlic
⅓ cup pine nuts
1 cup medium grain rice
1½ cups vegetable or chicken stock
⅓ cup currants
3 tablespoons each chopped fresh
parsley & mint
sea salt & freshly ground black pepper
½ cup white wine, stock or water

1　Heat a saucepan over a medium-low heat. Add a little oil, and the onion and garlic and cook for 5 minutes until onion is soft and translucent. Add pine nuts and cook for 5 minutes more.

2　Stir in rice and stock and bring to the boil. Cover pan and simmer gently for 10 minutes until all liquid has been absorbed. Stir in currants and herbs, and season with salt and pepper to taste.

(see photograph, page 94)

meat filling

olive oil
1 onion, finely diced
500g lamb mince
3 tablespoons finely chopped fresh basil
sea salt & freshly ground black pepper
⅓ cup pine nuts

serves 4

1　Heat a saucepan over a medium-low heat. Add a little oil and the onion and cook for 5 minutes until soft and translucent.

2　Raise the heat and add lamb mince to brown, stirring to break up any lumps of mince. Cook for 5 minutes or until most of the liquid has evaporated. Stir in basil, and season with salt and pepper to taste.

(see photograph, page 94)

THE IMAM FAINTED imam bayildi

An Ottoman legacy, *Imam bayildi* is one of the most famous dishes of Turkey. Translated, Imam bayildi means 'the Imam fainted' and there are several interpretations of how the dish got its name. Some say that when the Imam (a Muslim holy man or priest) first tasted this wonderful dish he swooned with pleasure because it was so delicious. Others say he fainted with shock when he saw how much expensive olive oil was used in the dish's preparation. Either way, a generous amount of unctuous olive oil is needed to give the stuffed eggplants their velvety soft texture and rich flavour.

96

6 medium-sized eggplants
(approximately 175g each)

sea salt & freshly ground black pepper

2 medium onions, sliced

2 tablespoons olive oil

4 cloves garlic, chopped

3 medium tomatoes,
peeled & coarsely sliced

2 teaspoons sugar

juice of 1 lemon

¼ cup chopped fresh parsley

½ cup water

½ cup olive oil

serves 6

1 Cut the stems from each eggplant. Peel lengthways strips at intervals around each eggplant to give a striped effect. Cut a deep slit on one side of each eggplant, almost from one end to the other. Season inside each slit with salt and pepper.

2 Heat a frying pan, add 3 tablespoonfuls of olive oil and lightly brown the eggplants on all sides. Remove to one side.

3 Add onions to the oil in the same pan and cook for 5–8 minutes until softened but not coloured. Add garlic and cook for 1 minute longer, then add tomatoes, sugar, lemon juice and parsley and stir to combine. Season with salt and pepper to taste. Preheat oven to 170°C.

4 Hold the slit of each eggplant open and spoon as much onion mixture as possible into the cavities. Arrange eggplants in a baking dish and spread any remaining filling mixture on top.

5 Add water and olive oil to the pan, then cover pan and bake for 50–60 minutes, or until eggplants are tender. Serve at room temperature.

(see photograph, page 95)

MOUSAKHA'A

Although the name of this recipe is the same as the Greek dish made with eggplant and minced lamb and topped with cheese, the combination of ingredients in this layered vegetable dish are unmistakably Middle Eastern. We ate Middle Eastern mousakha'a frequently during our travels – this is my interpretation of this sumptuous dish.

700g (2 medium) eggplants, trimmed

sea salt

olive oil

2 onions, finely sliced

1 green pepper, seeds removed, flesh finely sliced

3 cloves garlic, chopped

4 courgettes, trimmed & thickly sliced

700g medium tomatoes, peeled & chopped

1 cup labneh (see page 120)

3 eggs, lightly beaten

serves 6

1 Cut eggplants into 2cm cubes, place in a colander and sprinkle with salt. Leave to drain for 1 hour to remove bitter juices. Rinse with water, drain and dry on paper towels.

2 Heat a frying pan, add 2–3 tablespoons oil and the onion and green pepper. Cook over a medium heat for 10 minutes or until onion is softened and golden brown. Add garlic and cook for 1 minute more. Remove to a plate with a slotted spoon.

3 Now add eggplant to the pan, adding more oil if necessary and cook for 5–10 minutes, tossing frequently until golden brown. Remove to a plate and cook courgettes in the same way. Preheat oven to 180°C.

4 Arrange a layer of eggplant in the base of a large, deep-sided ovenproof dish (such as a lasagne dish). Cover with a layer of courgettes, then the onion and pepper mixture. Top with a layer of sliced tomatoes, seasoning with salt and pepper between layers.

5 Combine labneh with beaten eggs and spoon this mixture over the top of tomatoes. Bake for 30–40 minutes or until topping is golden brown and set.

THE NILE

Egypt is truly a land of contrasts where ruined temples sit beside new buildings; amusing street signs signal advice like present-day hieroglyphics; harsh desert is split by green oases; and contemporary tourists roam through ancient burial grounds. And through all of this flows the River Nile — the lifeblood of the country, without which Egypt could not exist.

We decide that a Nile cruise is the best way to see this river's important sites, to escape the tourist masses, and to enjoy the scenery of the Nile as we glide by in comfort and tranquillity. So we fly to Aswan and board Abercrombie and Kent's elegant *Sun Boat IV*. Immediately we are welcomed with tiny glasses of Middle Eastern lemonade and iced red hibiscus juice, loaded with sugar. Hibiscus juice, known as *karkadeeh*, is an infusion of hibiscus flowers, served hot or cold depending on the season. We settle into our cabins and prepare to give ourselves over to being pampered with beautiful meals, luxury travel and organised sightseeing excursions to ancient sites and monuments under the guidance of an Egyptologist.

Whenever possible, however, I like to leave the tourist trail and immerse myself in the crush of life within the local souks. The souks in Aswan and Luxor are some of the most astounding I have visited in the Middle East, yet they don't even rate a mention in most guidebooks.

Before we leave Aswan, I explore the lively souks situated just a couple of streets back from Corniche el Nil, the main road running along the riverbank. My walk from *Sun Boat IV* is intersected by the lively comings and goings along the Corniche; the calls of carriage drivers; feluccas setting sail; and a continual stream of deliveries of crates of raw produce to the cruise boats moored along the Nile.

Within the souks, spice stalls abound, exposing vibrant mounds of different-coloured spices — orange threads of saffron, burnt crimson paprika, bright red chilli powder, brownish cumin, yellow turmeric and vivid blue indigo. Although, strangely, always displayed beside the edible spices, indigo is used as a laundry agent to brighten white clothing and is sold in powdered form.

Just as striking are sacks of black dried limes, which impart a tart flavour when added to stews, and tacky clumps of brown tamarind pulp moulded into spherical shapes. And outside the poultry souk, live chickens are held upside down like shopping bags.

I particularly admire the distinctive handcrafted crates of latticed thin sticks that resemble birdcages. These contain tomatoes or aubergines or bright oranges complete with leaves. Rustic baskets hold all sorts of pulses and grains, or huge drifts of deep crimson, dried hibiscus flowers for making tea infusions. The pretty hand-woven baskets are also for sale. Virtually everything here is negotiable, from a kilo of oranges to an ornately sequinned belly-dancing outfit.

Street food is offered from makeshift stalls throughout the souks. I soon recognise a characteristic rounded pot on little burners containing broad beans stewed with spices, which Egyptians eat for breakfast slathered on pieces of sun bread with oil and lemon.

We leave Aswan and begin our cruise along the Nile. Breathtaking views of the raw Egyptian countryside pass before us. Willowy sugar cane, traditionally a major crop, lines the banks. Women carry vast loads of firewood on their heads. We pass clusters of mud houses divided by straw-lined animal stalls, and glimpse people going about their daily rituals at the water's edge, just as their ancestors have done for centuries.

The waterway is constantly churned by floating hotel boats, and feluccas slide by, their unique sails billowing as they catch the breeze that moves them along the water.

Naturally, we stop at important sites along the way to visit temples, such as Kom Ombo, the dual temple of the crocodile-god and the falcon-headed sky-god, and Edfu, where the Greek-built Temple of Horus still stands in a well-preserved state. In the dark of night we pass through the lock at Esna before motoring on towards Luxor.

In the kitchen, executive chef Ibrahim Rashed shares his recipes and cooking secrets as he introduces me to many authentic dishes. Today he is making the Egyptian pudding, *Um Ali*. Meaning Ali's mother, this dish is like a bread and butter pudding, made with pastry instead of bread, dotted with dried fruit and topped with a burnt cream crust. It is heavenly. In fact, all our banquets onboard *Sun Boat IV* are excellent, and most follow Egyptian or Oriental themes. Even though we eat three grand meals a day, I still can't wait to see what the kitchen will prepare next.

On the east bank of the Nile, the town of Luxor has only three main thoroughfares. I seek out the local souks a couple of roads back from Luxor's Corniche el Nil (behind the Avenue of Sphinxes standing guard over Luxor Temple). This time it's a little further to walk so I take a taxi, which in Aswan and Luxor comes in the form of a horse-drawn carriage, beautifully adorned with good-luck talismans – the hands of Fatima and evil eyes for protection. This seems a relatively safe option and such a ride is a priceless part of the Nile experience. The driver even offers to pick me up from a certain spot in two hours' time and drop me back to *Sun Boat IV*.

Navigating the winding medieval street cluttered with tiny stalls spilling over with foodstuffs and household necessities is exciting. A boisterous and time-honoured scene surrounds me. It's hot and the air is thick with noise and smells, and smoke billowing from charcoal grills.

I am drawn to the aroma of roasted sweet potatoes. This typical winter street-food is cooked in charcoal-fired ovens, complete with mini chimney-stacks, attached to donkey carts. I buy one to try. It is delivered into my hands wrapped in Arabic script newsprint, its warmth and burnt caramel flavour offering a comfort all its own.

Another curious treat available on the street is caramelised brown sugar cones. A vendor chases away insects attracted to his wares by waving a homemade fan of shredded newsprint tied up like a pom-pom. He smiles and offers me a taste. As I nibble a chunk of this crystalline creation I am surprised and delighted to recognise the familiar taste of hokey pokey.

The deeper into the souk I venture, the more interesting the displays become. Jostling side by side with Egyptians shopping for their daily essentials, I find myself the only non-local in sight. The occasional horse and cart pushes on through the compression of people in this extremely narrow street. Women swathed in black veils carry crates or bags of goods on their heads. Animated bartering can be seen and heard (even if not understood) outside every shop.

A welcome break comes at a coffee-house offering strong shots of sweet and sugary Egyptian tea or coffee. Tea invariably arrives in small battered teapots, and bunches of mint sit in vases of water on the table for tea drinkers to add, as preferred. I linger to watch an age-old scene unfolding, surrounded by men smoking *shisha* (hubbly bubbly water pipes) and children playing and eating sweet bread buns.

A perfume of antiquity seems to linger around old-fashioned fruits. Pomegranates, persimmons, velvety figs, dates, quinces, cherries and grapes all have distinct scents and tastes that contribute to the rich tapestry of Middle Eastern cuisine.

The pomegranate is a very old fruit believed to have originated in Persia or Afghanistan. Shrouded in history, myth and legend, some say the pomegranate was the original forbidden fruit found by Eve in the Garden of Eden. Boasting a sweet/tart flavour, which works well in sweet and savoury dishes alike, the concentrated juice of the pomegranate is also reduced to form pomegranate molasses, used in the preparation of many dressings, soups, stews and sauces. Delightful to look at, the gleaming seeds are used to adorn salads, dips such as hummus and baba ghanoush, puddings and other dishes.

We quickly develop the habit of ordering freshly squeezed pomegranate juice from juice bars all over the Middle East. There is a refreshing bite of bitter sweetness to this crimson-stained liquid, pressed from the jewel-like seeds. The juice of fresh guavas, large like apples, is also a popular choice.

In Turkey, I become addicted to a marvellous roast quince dessert. I return several times to Saray Muhallabicileri – a wonderfully old-fashioned milk-bar-cum-pudding-shop – situated on the shopping street of Istiklal Caddesi in Istanbul. The quinces served here have been roasted in thick sugar syrup so they caramelise and turn a striking deep crimson. Served with clotted cream, this fruit pudding is irresistible.

Throughout the Middle East clever use is made of every part of the grapevine. Fresh, ripe fruit is sold and eaten in all its simple splendour as a snack or for dessert. Raisins and golden sultanas are of course dried black and green grapes. Wine is made in some regions, such as Lebanon, Turkey and Egypt. Unripe grapes are pressed to make verjuice and sour grapes are pickled in vinegar and spices. And grape jam is popular as a spoon sweet. Even the vine leaves are eaten, fresh or preserved, and usually stuffed with rice or lamb.

Figs and dates can be found fresh and dried, and persimmons too, which when wizened look quite bizarre strung together like an edible necklace. Dates are often displayed still clustered on the stem. Life-sustaining in the desert, dates are considered a near-sacred fruit. Deliciously sweet thanks to sun-ripening, highly nutritious, and easy to transport – it's not surprising dates became the staple food of nomadic Arabs.

In Dubai, the capital of the United Arab Emirates, I meet a local Arab woman named Asma. Her warm dark eyes shine from under her veiled face, and her voice is strong and proud as she speaks to me of her history and her love of cooking.

'I only know my family's oral history back to my tenth great grandfather, but I know about my tribe – we are purely of Dubai,' she explains. 'This was never a green country – all we have is the sea and date palms. Our food is still simple and based on these ingredients – dates, fish, flour for bread, and later merchants brought basmati rice and spices from India.'

Dubai has rapidly risen from the desert to become one of the world's youngest yet most cosmopolitan cities. Key attractions are split between the historic and the ultramodern as rituals of the past and present continue side by side. Next to architectural glittering glass buildings are wharf scenes of cargo being unloaded by hand from traditional wooden boats and transported by horse and cart.

Just over forty years ago, life was simple in Dubai. In the beginning the country was poor – food was based on Bedouin cooking, the eating of ambulatory foods such as sheep, goats and camels, and transportable foods such as rice and dates.

Asma explains that there are hundreds of varieties of dates, some are better for eating fresh, and some are better for drying. A certain type are pressed through a funnel to extract the syrup and make date molasses.

'A good example of our food is a dish where rice is cooked with thick date syrup and served with fish fried in curry spices. This is a dish I like very much,' she says. Later, when I return to my hotel, Asma kindly sends me gifts of food so that I can taste all the ancestral dishes she has lovingly told me about.

EGYPTIAN CHICKEN WITH APRICOTS & FIGS morg polo

The inclusion of fruit in meat dishes is common in many Middle Eastern countries, where they have a preference for the mingling of savoury and sweet tastes. This is an Egyptian rendition, however, national borders do not confine flavours – by replacing the figs with olives, the dish would lean more towards the cuisine of Israel.

104

12 chicken thighs (with bone in)
sea salt & freshly ground black pepper
olive oil
I cup dried apricots
½ cup dried figs, halved
¼ cup raisins or sultanas
2 onions, finely sliced
2 teaspoons each ground
cinnamon & coriander
2½ cups chicken stock
1½ cups long grain rice

serves 6

1 Preheat oven to 190°C. Season chicken with salt and pepper. Heat a frying pan, add a little oil and brown chicken pieces for 2–3 minutes on each side. Remove to a roasting pan and scatter with apricots, figs and raisins.

2 In the same frying pan, cook onions over a gentle heat in a little more oil for 10 minutes until softened but not coloured. Add spices and fry for I minute. Add stock and bring to the boil, then pour this sauce over the chicken. Bake for 45 minutes.

3 Cook rice in boiling water for 10 minutes, then drain well. Season with salt and pepper and place in a buttered ovenproof dish. Spoon chicken and sauce on top. Cover with foil and bake for a further 30 minutes or until chicken tests cooked – when a sharp knife is inserted to the bone and the juices run clear.

4 Adjust seasoning of sauce with salt and pepper if necessary before serving.

PERSIAN LAMB & RHUBARB STEW Khoresh rivas

A *khoresh* is basically a casserole or stew — Persians consider it more of a stew-like sauce that is always served with fluffy steamed rice. Usually made with lamb, chicken or duck, these stews are modestly spiced but enriched with vegetables or exotic fruits, and tinged with sour juices that may come from citrus, pomegranate or verjuice. The khoresh is slow-cooked until the ingredients melt together and the meat is blissfully tender. Although western palates may find this a most unusual pairing, this delicious, sweet-sour lamb and rhubarb combination is typically Persian.

1kg boneless lamb shoulder steaks, trimmed of skin & fat

sea salt & freshly ground black pepper

3–4 tablespoons olive oil or clarified butter

2 large onions, finely sliced

pinch saffron threads, soaked in ¼ cup boiling water

1 tablespoon pomegranate molasses or juice of 1 lemon

2 cups beef or chicken stock

⅓ cup chopped fresh mint

⅓ cup chopped fresh flat-leaf parsley

500g rhubarb, trimmed

serves 6

1 Cut lamb into 3cm cubes and season with salt and pepper. Heat a flameproof casserole dish and brown lamb in 2–3 batches. Remove meat to one side and add onions to the pan with a little more oil if necessary. Cook onions over a medium heat for 10 minutes, stirring frequently until golden brown.

2 Return meat to the pan and add saffron and soaking liquid, pomegranate molasses or lemon juice and stock. Bring to the boil, then turn down the heat, cover pan and leave to simmer gently for 1 hour.

3 In a frying pan, fry mint and parsley in a little olive oil to release their flavour, tossing them quickly so they don't burn. Stir cooked herbs into lamb and continue to simmer stew uncovered for a further 30 minutes.

4 Cut rhubarb stalks into 3cm lengths. Add rhubarb to the casserole dish and simmer uncovered for 10 minutes to just cook rhubarb without pieces breaking up. Adjust seasoning of sauce with salt and pepper if necessary before serving with plain rice.

POMEGRANATE, FENNEL & CUCUMBER SALAD

Turkish cooks sometimes add grated fresh coconut to this refreshing salad combination. I like the addition of shaved fennel bulb, but finely shaved red onion could be substituted if preferred.

2 Lebanese cucumbers, peeled
2 tablespoons extra virgin olive oil
sea salt & freshly ground black pepper
2 small fennel bulbs, trimmed
juice of 2 lemons
2 pomegranates
½ cup torn fresh mint leaves

serves 4-6

1 Quarter cucumbers lengthways, then slice and place in a large bowl. Drizzle with olive oil and season with salt and pepper.

2 Very finely slice fennel bulbs, place in another bowl and toss with lemon juice to stop the fennel from discolouring.

3 Cut or break open pomegranates to remove the edible seeds, discard pith and skin.

4 Combine fennel and lemon juice in the bowl with cucumber and toss well. Sprinkle over pomegranate seeds and garnish with torn mint leaves.

106

PERSIAN DUCK WITH POMEGRANATE & WALNUT SAUCE
fesenjân

Fesenjân is an ancient and classic dish that remains popular in Iran, where it is invariably served at all religious festival dinners. Fesenjân is a khoresh or stew that can be made of duck, chicken, lamb or veal, or sometimes fish or ground meat. I find the duck version most pleasing — there is something about this thick and richly dark, sour, nutty sauce that perfectly complements the decadent fattiness of duck.

250g toasted walnut pieces

6 whole duck legs

sea salt & freshly ground black pepper

1 large onion, finely diced

1 tablespoon ground cinnamon

3 tablespoons soft brown sugar

¼ cup pomegranate molasses

2½ cups chicken stock

seeds of 1 pomegranate or ½ cup toasted walnuts, coarsely chopped to garnish

¼ cup coarsely chopped fresh mint to garnish

serves 6

1 Finely grind walnuts in a food processor. Season duck with salt and pepper.

2 Heat a flameproof casserole dish, add duck legs, skin-side down, and cook for 5 minutes to brown. There is no need to add oil to the pan as the duck will cook in its own fat. Turn duck over and brown the other side, then remove to one side.

3 Pour off any excess fat, leaving 2 tablespoons in the pan. Add onion and cook over a medium heat for 5–10 minutes or until softened and golden brown. Add cinnamon, sugar and ground walnuts and cook for 1 minute, stirring continuously. Now add pomegranate molasses and chicken stock and bring sauce to the boil.

4 Add duck legs and baste with sauce. Turn down the heat, cover pan and gently simmer for 1¼ hours.

5 Skim off any fat as it rises to the surface and adjust seasoning of sauce with salt and pepper, if necessary. Serve duck legs coated in sauce and garnished with pomegranate seeds or walnuts and chopped mint. Plainly cooked long grain rice is an appropriate accompaniment for this rich dish.

SOUR CHERRY SAUCE WITH MEATBALLS lahm bil karaz

This medieval Arabic recipe originated in Northern Syria and similar versions also come from Iran, where cherry trees bear fruit in profusion. Once again this dish shows the Middle Eastern predilection for unusual pairings of meat and fruit. In the winter, dried sour cherries are used in place of fresh.

700g lamb or beef mince

3 cloves garlic, crushed

I teaspoon ground coriander

½ teaspoon each ground allspice, cloves & cinnamon

sea salt & freshly ground black pepper

olive oil for frying

sour cherry sauce (recipe below)

3 tablespoons toasted pine nuts to garnish

1 Combine mince, garlic and spices in a bowl and knead or pound until blended into a smooth paste. Season well with salt and pepper.

2 With damp hands, mould 24 walnut-sized portions into balls and set aside on a tray.

3 Heat oil in a large frying pan and fry meatballs until golden brown all over (this will need to be done in 2–3 batches). Return all meatballs to the pan.

4 Pour cherry sauce over browned meatballs, then simmer on the stovetop for 10 minutes, stirring regularly to prevent sticking. Serve scattered with pine nuts.

sour cherry sauce

300g fresh cherries, halved & pitted (or substitute ¾ cup dried sour cherries)

I–2 tablespoons liquid honey, to taste

juice of I lemon

I teaspoon ground cinnamon

I cup water

sea salt & freshly ground black pepper

1 Heat a large saucepan, add cherries, honey, lemon juice, cinnamon and water and bring to the boil. Reduce heat to a gentle simmer and cook for 10–15 minutes, stirring often until the cherries are tender. Season with salt and pepper to taste.

serves 4

110

TURKISH ROAST QUINCE WITH CLOTTED CREAM

Cultivated in the Eastern Mediterranean for centuries, the ancient quince is still popularly preserved and enjoyed throughout the region. We ate this heavenly dessert in a café in Istanbul, Turkey, and found it so alluring that we returned several times for another taste of this sweet treat. As the quinces cook in a thick sugar syrup, they magically turn from pale golden to deep ruby red and release the most beautiful perfume. The finished candied fruit was served to us topped with a luscious dollop of Middle Eastern clotted cream — beware, this combination is truly addictive.

3 cups sugar

1 cinnamon stick

2 cups water

pared rind and juice of 1 lemon

3 quinces, peeled, halved & cored

clotted cream to serve (I find Italian mascarpone makes a good substitute if necessary)

serves 6

1 Preheat oven to 180°C. Place sugar, cinnamon stick, water, lemon zest and juice in a large saucepan. Bring to the boil, stirring until the sugar dissolves.

2 Place quince halves in a roasting pan to fit snugly. Pour hot sugar syrup and spices over quinces. Cover pan with foil and bake for 3 hours until quince halves have turned dark pink and are tender, basting regularly. The longer the fruit cooks, the darker in colour it will become.

3 Remove covering foil and baste quinces with syrup from the pan. Return to the oven for 1 hour or until quinces are lightly caramelised on the surface.

4 Remove to a deep-sided dish with a slotted spoon. Drizzle quince with remaining cooking syrup and refrigerate until cold. Serve chilled topped with clotted cream.

111

DRIED FIG & ANISEED JAM

The Arabs make many different kinds of jam. While these jams resemble those made in the West, they are often used in different ways. For instance, jam will be eaten by the spoonful as a spoon sweet, or added by the spoonful to a glass of hot tea.

Mastic is not usually available outside the Middle East. It is a wonderfully aromatic and exotic flavouring, but not essential to the perfect finished consistency of this jam. So, if it cannot be procured, don't fret as this jam will still be delightful.

1kg dried figs

1kg sugar

2 teaspoons aniseeds

3 tablespoons lemon juice

1 cup cold water

¼ cup toasted sesame seeds

1 teaspoon cinnamon

1 teaspoon ground mastic (optional)

makes 900ml

1 Wash dried figs to remove any grit. Dry on paper towels, then coarsely chop. Place sugar, aniseeds, lemon juice and water in a heavy-based saucepan and bring to the boil, stirring until sugar dissolves.

2 Add chopped figs and boil over high heat for 5 minutes, then lower the heat and simmer for another 30 minutes. Lastly stir in sesame seeds, cinnamon and mastic (if available), then remove pan from heat and set aside to cool a little for 10 minutes so that fruit is evenly distributed.

3 Pour jam into hot, sterilised jars and seal well.

DATE PASTRIES ma'amoul

Ma'amoul, a type of moulded biscuit filled with dates or sometimes a mixture of ground walnuts, are a great favourite of mine. We found versions of these date pastries in many different countries — they are even served in-flight with Arabic coffee on some Middle Eastern airlines. Specially patterned wooden moulds for shaping ma'amoul are sold in the souks, however, these biscuits can be left as plain rounds if you don't have a specialised mould. Patterned or plain, ma'amoul are irresistible.

filling

10g butter

150g pitted dates, coarsely chopped

¾ cup cold water

1 teaspoon rose water
or orange flower water

pastry

1 cup fine semolina

1 cup plus 2 tablespoons plain flour

¼ teaspoon baking powder

½ cup caster sugar

1 teaspoon rose water
or orange flower water

200g butter, melted

icing sugar to dust

makes 16

1 Place all ingredients, except floral water, in a saucepan and bring to the boil. Turn down heat and simmer gently, stirring frequently and mashing mixture with a wooden spoon, until dates soften and liquid reduces leaving a thick paste. Stir in floral water and transfer to a bowl to cool.

1 Combine semolina, flour, baking powder, sugar, rose or orange flower water and butter in a bowl and mix thoroughly. Turn dough out on a work surface and lightly knead to bring together and form a smooth dough. Rest pastry for 30 minutes.

2 Meanwhile, preheat oven to 180°C and line a baking tray with non-stick baking paper. Divide pastry mixture into 16 portions. Take a portion of pastry and flatten this into a disc. Place a teaspoonful of cold date filling in the centre of the disc, then bring the edges together to enclose filling and mould to form a smooth ball.

3 Repeat process until you have 16 filled balls. Place these on the prepared baking tray and press to slightly flatten each ball. Or, if you have a biscuit mould, press each ball into the mould and release to leave a pretty imprint in the top of each biscuit.

4 Bake for 20–30 minutes or until pale golden (not brown). Remove to a wire rack to cool and dust with icing sugar. Ma'amoul will keep in an airtight container for several weeks.

(see photograph, page 114)

113

CHOCOLATE-DIPPED FIGS & DATES ON CRYSTALLISED ROSE PETALS

Figs and dates stuffed with almonds or almond paste (marzipan) are common delicacies in many Middle Eastern countries. I have gone one step further and dipped these sweetmeats in a chocolate coating. While chocolate is an unconventional ingredient in Middle Eastern cooking, this small novelty, a blend of Middle Eastern and Western flavours, is one that I enjoy. Similarly, I have played with the Middle Eastern concept of edible rose petals, dusting these in a sugary veil so that they form crisp receptacles for the chocolate fruit to fill.

116

10 soft dessert figs

10 fresh dates, pitted

20 blanched almonds

250g dark chocolate roughly chopped, to dip

crystallised rose petals (recipe on next page)

makes 20

1 Wipe figs and dates with paper towels (especially if they have been softened with water because any moisture will prevent the chocolate coating from adhering, or cause the moisture to weep through and break down the chocolate coating).

2 Cut a small slit in the bottom (not the stalk end) of each fig and insert an almond through this slit into the centre of each fig. Place an almond inside each date from where the stone was taken.

3 Place chocolate to melt in a bowl set over a saucepan of steaming water, stirring until chocolate is smooth and liquid, or microwave in short bursts.

4 Holding the stem of each fig, or holding a skewer threaded through the stem end, dip each fig in the melted chocolate to coat. Remove to a tray lined with non-stick baking paper. Dip the dates in the melted chocolate and remove to the tray with a skewer or a spoon.

5 Leave figs and dates in a cool place to set. Sit each chocolate-dipped fig or date on a crystallised rose petal to serve.

crystallised rose petals

2 large perfumed, pink or red roses
I egg white, lightly beaten
I cup caster sugar

1 Remove roses from stems and separate petals.
Place sugar over the surface of a plate.

2 With an artist's brush, lightly paint a rose petal
with egg white, then gently toss petal in sugar to
lightly coat.

3 Place sugar-coated rose petal on a tray lined
with greaseproof paper. Repeat process until all
petals are sugar coated. Set tray of petals in a warm
dry place for 2—3 days until firm, dry and crisp.
Store in an airtight container separated by sheets
of greaseproof paper.

(see photograph, page 115)

curds
& whey
yoghurt, milk
cream, cheese

Yoghurt drained of its whey forms a delectable substance known in Arabic as labneh. Often referred to as strained yoghurt cheese, labneh has a gorgeous milky sweet/tart flavour and a thick cream cheese consistency. I still have the taste of true labneh on my tongue — it has a texture and flavour that cannot be precisely reproduced outside its homeland and remains an indelible taste memory.

Our days in the Middle East are punctuated by food, starting with breakfast and moving on to a continual feast of tastes. Each morning I am presented with a tempting Oriental breakfast of pita bread, luscious labneh and accompaniments. The labneh arrives in a shallow bowl and splashed with rich green extra virgin olive oil. This is perfect to dip or spread on piles of warm pita bread and top with sliced tomato, sliced fresh Lebanese cucumber and pickled cucumber too. There's also an assortment of other cheeses: salted feta-style cheese and halloumi, and another white cheese, along with a huge bunch of fresh mint on the side.

Legend has it that the first cheese was made in the Middle East. It's believed to be the result of one of those accidents that led to something wonderful. The story goes that an Arab nomad filled a saddlebag with milk to sustain him on a long journey across the desert by camel. The heat of the sun and the movement of the animal caused the milk to separate into curds and whey. When the nomad opened his saddlebag he discovered a soft white mass and found this was edible and even quite tasty. From these strange and humble beginnings, cheese has developed into a thoroughly appetising foodstuff.

But cheese is a very curious food when you think about it, as essentially it is produced by subjecting milk to the controlled action of spoilage, which changes it from a liquid into a solid substance. This solid may then go on to be pressed, aged, or perhaps left to sit in salty brine, as is the case with feta cheese.

Unfortunately I don't know the name for the most extraordinary cheese I've ever come across. I found this cheese in Azerbaijan, but I believe a similar type, known as *tulum*, is made in Turkey. The cheese is cured in the full skin of the goat, from whence I presume the milk came. The skin must be treated in some way and cleaned, then filled with the curds and left to cure and mature. The solid bloated mass of cheese-filled goatskin all stitched together and tried up with string makes a weird display in the cheese shop. Amounts of the dry-textured cheese are scraped out to order. I imagine this is a local delicacy. I am given a smidgen to taste — it is dry and crumbly with a bitingly sharp, almost acrid taste. I don't go back for seconds.

Cheese in this part of the world is commonly made following traditional ways, mostly from the milk of goats and sheep, but also from cows. There is a huge selection of cheeses to choose from and many vary from region to region and even from village to village. Everyday cheeses include a fresh white cheese in curd form, similar to Italian ricotta, which is often eaten for breakfast, as a snack, or as mezze. Pressed, this white cheese is commonly salted and preserved in brine, in the style of feta. Halloumi is another popular cheese, originating in Cyprus but found in many Middle Eastern countries. It is a stretched curd cheese also preserved in brine, with a firm chewy texture, and is often served sliced and fried. Various cheeses are also used in cooking, to stuff vegetables, top breads, and fill pastries, both savoury and sweet.

One other dairy product that needs to be mentioned is butter. Clarified butter is the classic cooking fat or shortening of the Middle East, where it is known as *samneh*. This is the same ingredient used in the cooking of India, where it is known as ghee. Samneh is simple to make and it keeps well because when the solids are removed from butter it lasts longer, even in the hot climate.

STRAINED YOGHURT CHEESE labneh

This strained yoghurt cheese is also known by the Middle Eastern name of labneh. The longer the yoghurt is strained, the firmer the cheese becomes. Soft labneh is often served at breakfast. Firm labneh can be rolled into cheese balls. These balls can be dipped in herbs, seeds or spices but they also make an excellent accompaniment to salads and spicy dishes.

large square of fine muslin or cheesecloth

4 cups natural unsweetened yoghurt

I teaspoon sea salt

makes 2 cups

120

1   Sterilise a piece of muslin or cheesecloth big enough to line a large bowl by boiling in a saucepan of water for 5 minutes. Remove and rinse with cold water to cool, then squeeze out excess moisture.

2   Spread muslin inside a large bowl. Pour yoghurt into the centre of the muslin-lined bowl. Bring the four corners of muslin cloth together and tie these around a wooden spoon. Suspend the spoon over the bowl, refrigerate and allow the yoghurt to drain into the bowl for I–3 days.

3   After one day the yoghurt cheese is thick and spreadable. After 3 days the yoghurt cheese becomes firm and can be rolled into balls, which will keep for about 10 days in the fridge marinated in olive oil.

FILO PASTRY CIGARS FILLED WITH CHEESE *sigara böreği*

Börek are Turkish pastries, made in a huge assortment and profusion but the most commonly known variety are these little rolls shaped like cigars or fingers and filled with white cheese. The pastry may vary, sometimes being more like a Tunisian brick pastry or Moroccan *wharka*, however, the modern cook will find that *phyllo* (filo) is the most widely available and will work perfectly for these appetising savoury pastries. *Börek* are fried or steamed but I like these baked versions best of all.

200g feta cheese, crumbled
1 egg, lightly beaten
3 tablespoons chopped fresh parsley
1 tablespoon chopped fresh mint
4 sheets filo pastry
50g butter, melted

makes 12

1 Combine feta, egg and herbs in a bowl and mix well. Preheat oven to 190°C.

2 Lay a sheet of filo pastry on a work surface and brush lightly with melted butter. Place another sheet on top, cut this into 6 even-sized squares. Repeat with the remaining 2 sheets of filo, so you end up with 12 squares.

3 Butter edges of a square of filo. Take 1 tablespoon of filling mixture and place in a sausage shape at one end of the pastry. Fold in 1cm along both sides of pastry to secure filling and roll up like a cigar. Repeat with remaining squares of filo until you have 12 cigar rolls.

4 Place all the rolls on a baking tray and brush outer surface lightly with butter. Bake for 15–20 minutes or until golden brown. Serve hot.

YOGHURT & LENTIL SOUP

Soups are often found as a street-food breakfast dish, sold by vendors in the early morning. This simple soup appears quite elaborate because of its novel presentation.

150g burghul wheat
150g red lentils
4 cups chicken or vegetable stock
3 tablespoons olive oil
2 onions, finely diced
½ cup tomato purée
1 red chilli, seeds removed, flesh chopped
sea salt and freshly ground black pepper
1 cup plain yoghurt
2 tablespoons chopped fresh
mint to garnish

serves 4

1 Place burghul wheat in a bowl, cover with cold water and leave to soak for 15 minutes, then drain well.

2 Place lentils in a saucepan, cover with stock and bring to the boil. Turn down the heat and simmer for 20 minutes. Add drained burghul wheat and continue cooking for another 10 minutes, adding a little water when necessary. When lentils are tender and soup is thick, season with salt and pepper to taste.

3 At the same time, heat a saucepan, add oil and onion and cook over a moderate heat for 10 minutes until onion has softened but not coloured. Add tomato purée and simmer for 5 minutes. Add chilli and season with salt and pepper to taste.

4 To serve, ladle lentil soup into soup bowls, spoon tomato mixture into the centre and then some yoghurt, so that 3 concentric rings form. Garnish with mint.

SLOW-COOKED OTTOMAN LAMB MARINATED IN YOGHURT

Long, slow cooking leaves this meat meltingly tender. Don't be disappointed that the lamb is no longer pink, as it will be as succulent as you could ever wish lamb to be. The spicy yoghurt marinade forms a thick, flavoursome blanket over the lamb and infuses the meat with aromatics.

1.5kg leg of lamb,
trimmed of skin & fat

5 cloves garlic, cut in slivers

yoghurt marinade

1 cup natural unsweetened yoghurt

finely grated zest & juice of 1 lemon

¼ cup olive oil

3 tablespoons tomato paste

¼ teaspoon chilli powder

½ teaspoon ground allspice

sea salt & freshly ground black pepper

serves 8

1 With the tip of a sharp knife, make deep thin slits all over lamb meat, then insert slivers of garlic into each incision. Place lamb in a large ceramic dish.

2 Combine marinade ingredients and rub all over lamb. Cover with plastic wrap and refrigerate overnight to marinate.

3 Remove lamb from fridge and bring to room temperature. Preheat oven to 210°C. Transfer lamb to a roasting pan, leaving yoghurt coating intact. Cook lamb for 30 minutes until a golden crust forms. Reduce temperature to 150°C and continue baking for 2 hours.

4 Remove lamb from oven, cover with a tent of foil and rest for 15 minutes, then slice to serve.

YOGHURT & CUCUMBER SAUCE caçik

Caçik is the Turkish name for this yoghurt and cucumber sauce, however, it is popular throughout the Middle East. It tastes wonderful eaten plain but warm pita bread is the obvious accompaniment. As a sauce, this combination also works well over grilled fish, vegetables or meats.

2 Lebanese cucumbers

1 cup thick natural unsweetened yoghurt

2 cloves garlic, crushed

2 tablespoons extra virgin olive oil

juice of 1 lemon

3 tablespoons chopped fresh mint

sea salt

makes 2 cups

1 Halve cucumbers and remove seeds by running a teaspoon down the central seed canal. Discard seeds. Finely dice cucumber flesh and place in a colander. Sprinkle with salt and leave to drain over a bowl for 30 minutes.

1 Rinse cucumber in cold water, drain well, then dry on paper towels. Mix cucumber with yoghurt, garlic, olive oil, lemon juice and mint. Season with salt to taste.

pOTATO SALAD WiTH YOGHURT & DiLL DRESSiNG

Yoghurt is the obvious base to form a creamy dressing for this Middle Eastern potato salad.

2 Lebanese cucumbers
sea salt
500g (3 medium-sized) waxy potatoes
freshly ground black pepper
½ cup thick unsweetened natural yoghurt
3 tablespoons extra virgin olive oil
¼ cup finely chopped fresh dill

serves 4

1 Halve cucumbers and remove seeds by running a teaspoon down the central seed canal. Discard seeds. Grate cucumber flesh and place in a colander. Sprinkle with salt and leave to drain over a bowl for 30 minutes, then rinse cucumber in cold water and squeeze to remove excess moisture.

2 At the same time, cook potatoes whole in boiling salted water until tender. Drain well then peel and coarsely chop. Toss warm chopped potatoes and prepared cucumber together in a large bowl. Season with pepper and extra salt if needed.

3 Mix together yoghurt, olive oil and chopped dill to form a dressing. Pour dressing over salad ingredients and toss well. Serve warm.

ORIENTAL RICE PUDDING riz bi-haleeb

This perfumed and nourishing milk and rice pudding is very popular throughout the Middle East. As with most home-cooked dishes, each cook will have his or her own preferred version. This is my favourite combination of flavourings.

½ cup short grain rice

4 cups milk, plus extra if necessary

1 cup water

½ cup sugar

finely grated zest of ½ lemon

2 teaspoons rose water or orange flower water, as preferred

¼ cup cream

½ teaspoon cinnamon, to serve

serves 4

1 Wash rice really well in running cold water. Place rice in a saucepan with milk, water, sugar and lemon zest and bring to the boil. Then lower the heat and gently simmer for 25 minutes until rice is tender and coated in a creamy sauce. A little more milk may need to be added to bring rice to a cooked consistency.

2 Stir in rose or orange flower water and cream, then remove to a serving bowl or individual bowls. Refrigerate until cold. Serve sprinkled with cinnamon.

milk pudding muhallabiah

Individual bowls of this classic milk custard pudding are sold in sweet stores throughout the Middle East. The velvety pudding may be topped with chopped pistachio nuts or almonds, drenched in rose water and strewn with rose petals, or dotted with fruit preserves. I choose to adorn my *muhallabiah* with a luscious nut and pomegranate seed syrup (see page 81), as the taste and texture complements this creamy pudding beautifully.

1 cup cream

2 cups full cream milk

¾ cup sugar

1 cup blanched almonds, finely ground

2 drops almond extract

2 tablespoons cornflour

serves 4

1 Place cream, milk, sugar, ground almonds and almond extract in a saucepan and bring to the boil. Remove to stand for 20 minutes for the almond flavour to infuse into the milk.

2 Strain mixture through a fine sieve, pressing hard on the almonds with the back of a spoon to remove as much moisture as possible. Discard almonds and return liquid to the pan.

3 Dissolve cornflour in a little of the reserved liquid and add this to the pan. Return the pan to a medium heat and cook, stirring frequently until the mixture thickens to coat the back of the spoon.

4 Pour into individual glasses or *ramekins* and chill to serve.

um ali

Varying from country to country and cook to cook, we tasted many different renditions of this classic pudding. The more I tasted, the more fascinated I became with this pudding of unique taste and texture.

Um Ali, meaning Ali's mother, is just the kind of pudding a mother would make with warmth and affection. It is reminiscent of English bread and butter pudding but made with pastry instead of bread. Some versions are flavoured delicately with rose water. This is the best recipe I tasted in all my travels and I thank Egyptian chef Ibrahim Rashed for sharing the secrets of his Um Ali with me.

130

320g puff pastry

¼ cup slivered pistachio nuts or almonds

¼ cup raisins

4 cups full cream milk

¼ cup sugar

2 tablespoons honey

I teaspoon ground cinnamon

½ cup cream, lightly whipped

icing sugar to dust

serves 4

1 Preheat oven to 220°C. Line two baking sheets with non-stick baking paper. On a lightly floured surface, roll out puff pastry to 3mm thick. Cut into large portions to fit the size of the baking tray (no need to be precise as they will be broken up later). Place pastry on prepared baking sheets. Prick all over with a fork and bake for 15–20 minutes or until puffed and golden brown. Remove to a wire rack to cool.

2 Break up cooked pastry and place pieces into 4 individual ovenproof dishes or one large deep-sided ovenproof dish, alternating layers with a sprinkling of nuts and raisins.

3 In a saucepan, heat milk, sugar, honey and cinnamon to just below boiling point, stirring until sugar dissolves. Pour hot mixture over pastry, then leave to soak for 5 minutes.

4 Preheat a grill. Top the pudding with whipped cream, dust with icing sugar and grill for 2–5 minutes or until sugar caramelises, then serve.

the,
**baker's
oven** bread, flatbread,
fillings, toppings

Burnished-brown flatbreads emerge from the baker's oven. The inviting scent of hot bread emanates from the bakery and out into the street attracting a line of hungry purchasers. This scene is repeated time and again as we are taken on a night-time tour of Bahrain's most interesting specialised bakeries.

One man buries his hands in a big bowl of flour; another shapes the dough, rolling it thinly with practised hands. Yet another slaps the rounds onto the inside of the flaming hot oven, or picks the cooked flatbreads off with a metal skewer. This evening ritual follows the production of a simple necessity – slightly leavened rustic flatbread baked in a tandoor-style oven. Tandoor-baked bread is also common in Turkey, Iran and Afghanistan. Like all bread it varies a great deal from country to country, and even from baker to baker.

Different bakeries on our tour proudly produce certain speciality breads. Highly prized is date bread, composed of flour, a little yeast and date syrup made from dates soaked in boiling water then strained. I am given a round of date bread to taste – it's sweet and a little nutty with a lovely caramel flavour from the dates. I'm told that sometimes sesame seeds or aniseeds are added to the mix for special celebration days.

The classic flatbread most associated with the Middle East is pita bread. But there are many different and interesting kinds of bread produced here, from unleavened mountain breads to sweet bread buns. There are thin nomadic breads, and thicker breads, such as Turkish pide and Egyptian sun bread.

In Beirut, Lebanon, a delicious scent of caramelised flour captures my attention and demands a closer inspection. In a rudimentary storefront set-up, over a dome-shaped hotplate, the most fantastic flatbread is being produced. This is *saj* – paper-thin, dry, almost crêpe-like bread that is slathered with olive oil and sprinkled with za'atar. We are shyly and unceremoniously given samples, which are rolled up in paper for take-out purposes. We nibble our gift of aromatic bread and wander back along the darkening street towards our hotel.

During our Nile cruise, we find stacks of unusual-looking loaves in both Aswan and Luxor. This is *eesh shamsi* or sun bread – so-called because it is left to rise in the hot sun. But don't go looking for it in Cairo as it is only made in Upper Egypt. I'm told that sun bread is reputed to be the best bread in Egypt and compares favourably with French *pain au levain*. I buy a loaf to taste. It is golden brown with a crispy crust, a slightly sour flavour and a marvellously moist and chewy bite.

Still in Egypt, we discover Cairo is a city bursting at the seams. While Egypt's ancient monuments, ruins, temples, pyramids and tombs entice the majority of tourists to visit this fascinating land, we find the Egyptian capital city is well worth exploring in its own right.

After visiting a small and interesting step pyramid at Sakara, which is less known and much more peaceful than the Great Pyramids of Giza, we drive back towards Cairo past houses with bright naïve paintings on their walls that tell stories of pilgrimage trips made to Mecca. We stop at a restaurant for lunch where the speciality is spit roast whole chicken accompanied by amazingly fresh flatbread. In fact, it is so fresh they are making the bread before our eyes. A large group of women sitting on the ground, rolling dough out on boards, surround a wood-fired oven, while puffed hot pillows of pita are removed from the baker's oven as we watch.

Bread is the staple part of any meal. The Middle Eastern custom is to eat from a common dish, and so bread is used, in a way, as edible cutlery. Small pieces ripped from the loaf are held with the fingers like pincers and used to gather mouthfuls of dips and spreads, to sop up juices, to dip into soups, and to wipe the plate clean of any last drop of flavour.

There are also many different uses for stale bread, which may be added to thicken soups and stews, to bind meatballs, or to drench in sugar syrup to form a dessert. And for centuries now, Middle Eastern cooks have been tossing together fresh seasonal vegetables, a fragrant lemony dressing and yesterday's bread to form an irresistible salad called fattoush.

PITA BREAD khubz

Bread is called *khubz* in Arabic. There are many different recipes for bread, but flat pita bread is the traditional type of bread that is most well known outside the Middle East.

Some restaurants make their own fresh bread – light pillows of hot pita bread fresh from the oven is one of the most simple but best tastes imaginable. I like to make my pita bread with a mixture of plain and whole-wheat flour, as this gives the bread more flavour and texture. Cook pita bread on a pizza stone if you have one as this gives a more authentic result, otherwise use a hot oven tray.

134

¼ cup lukewarm water

pinch sugar

I teaspoon active dry yeast

I cup lukewarm water

I cup whole-wheat flour

2 cups plain flour, plus extra for kneading & rolling

I teaspoon salt

I tablespoon olive oil

makes 6–12

1 Place ¼ cup lukewarm water in a small bowl and sprinkle with sugar and yeast. Set aside in a warm place for 5–10 minutes until the mixture foams, indicating that the yeast is activated.

2 Place this activated yeast mixture and I cup lukewarm water in a large bowl. Sift together flours and mix half the flour mixture into yeast and water to form a smooth paste. Set this mixture (called the sponge) in a warm place for 30 minutes to rise.

3 Add salt and olive oil to the sponge, then mix in remaining flour, working the mixture into a moist but firm dough. Turn dough out onto a lightly floured surface and knead for 5–8 minutes, or until smooth and elastic. Lightly oil the bowl and return dough to the bowl. Cover bowl with a damp cloth or plastic wrap and set in a warm place for dough to rise for I hour or until doubled in volume.

4 Place an oven tray or pizza stone in the oven and preheat oven to 220°C. Divide dough into 6 equal portions and roll each portion into a ball. Either roll out with a rolling pin or hand press each ball of dough into a 5mm thick, 10cm disk. Place circles in the oven onto hot baking trays or pizza stone and bake for 8–10 minutes, or until the pita are puffed and light golden brown.

5 Alternatively, divide dough into 12 equal portions to make smaller rounds and cook for 6–8 minutes.

FLATBREAD PIZZA WITH THYME *manaqish bil-za'atar*

Olive oil and za'atar forms a simple but traditional topping for flatbread baked in the oven. This topping is also used on another type of flatbread called *saj*, which is more like a crisp shell of pastry-like bread cooked over a dome-shaped hot-plate heated by a charcoal or gas fire. We ate many versions of this flavoured bread throughout Lebanon, often for breakfast or as a street-food snack. I also enjoyed a version where halloumi or feta-style cheese is included with the za'atar topping.

I recipe pita bread dough (see page 134)

olive oil

I recipe za'atar (see page 42)

makes 6–12

1 Make bread dough and leave to double in volume. Preheat oven to 220°C.

2 Divide dough into 6–12 portions, depending on size desired. Roll dough into 5mm thick discs, place on a baking tray and brush with oil and scatter with za'atar. Bake for 4–8 minutes.

LAMB & HUMMUS FLATBREAD PIZZA lahma bi ajeen

These wonderfully thin flatbreads topped with lamb could be thought of as Middle Eastern pizzas. Different renditions of these Arab-style pizzas can be found throughout the Middle East. With a topping of minced lamb, these are called *lahma bi ajeen* in Lebanon. Pine nuts, sumac, parsley or onions may be scattered over the top. In Turkey, these pizzas are known as *lahmacun*, where the lamb mixture may contain tomato. I like to add a saucy topping of creamy hummus and torn fragrant herbs that release their perfume with the warmth of the pizza.

1 recipe pita bread dough (see page 134)
olive oil
hummus (see page 20)
¼ cup torn fresh coriander leaves
¼ cup torn fresh mint leaves

lamb topping
1 tablespoon olive oil
1 onion, finely diced
2 cloves garlic, chopped
375g lean lamb mince
¼ teaspoon each ground allspice
& chilli powder
juice of 1 lemon
sea salt & freshly ground black pepper
3 tablespoons pine nuts

makes 6

1 Heat a frying pan, add oil, onion and garlic and cook over a medium-high heat for 5 minutes until onion is softened and golden brown. Add lamb and cook until browned. Drain off any excess fat.

2 Add spices and lemon juice and cook for 2–3 minutes more. Season with salt and pepper to taste. Set mixture aside to cool.

3 Divide bread dough into 6 portions and roll out to form 5mm-thick oval lengths or discs of a size that will fit onto your oven trays. Brush flatbreads with oil and scatter with lamb topping leaving the outer edges free of topping. Sprinkle with pine nuts and bake for 7–10 minutes or until golden brown.

4 Remove flatbreads from oven, dollop with hummus and scatter with herbs. Serve immediately.

5 Alternatively, make mini pita pizzas, if preferred.

137

AZERBAIJANI KUTAP WITH HERB OR PUMPKIN FILLING

Kutap is a wonderful filled, paper-thin flatbread that is cooked in a skillet as opposed to in the oven. We tried both fillings, one herbal and one of pumpkin purée – both were very special. After intricate demonstration, cousins Sevinj Aliyeva and Chimna Aliyeva passed this recipe to me.

¼ cup lukewarm water

pinch sugar

½ teaspoon dried yeast

2 cups flour, sifted,
plus extra for kneading & rolling

I teaspoon salt

I tablespoon oil

extra lukewarm water to mix

makes 12

138

1 Place ¼ cup lukewarm water in a small bowl and sprinkle with sugar and yeast. Set aside in a warm place for 5–10 minutes until the mixture foams indicating that the yeast is activated.

2 Place flour and salt in a large bowl. Add oil and activated yeast mixture and mix this in by hand, adding extra lukewarm water bit by bit until a firm but elastic dough forms. Turn dough out onto a lightly floured surface and knead for 5 minutes until smooth. Lightly oil bowl. Place dough in bowl and cover with a damp cloth or with plastic wrap and set aside in a warm place for 30 minutes to rise.

3 Punch back dough with your fist and knead lightly. Divide dough into small balls. Roll each ball out as thinly as possible to form a circle. Spread half the circle with chosen filling ingredients and season with salt and pepper. Fold dough over to form a half circle and to enclose the filling. Crimp edges into a scallop shape to seal.

4 Heat a large heavy-based frying pan or skillet. Place I or 2 kutap in the hot dry pan and cook for 3–5 minutes on each side or until golden brown.

herbal filling

½ cup fresh coriander leaves

½ cup fresh parsley leaves

¼ cup fresh chervil leaves

¼ cup fresh dill leaves

I cup baby spinach leaves

1 Roughly chop all herbs and spinach and combine in a bowl. Toss well and use to fill kutap, as directed.

139

pumpkin purée filling

¼ large pumpkin, seeds removed & peeled

olive oil

1 Preheat oven to 200°C. Cut pumpkin flesh into coarse chunks. Place in a roasting pan and drizzle with olive oil.

2 Roast for 30 minutes or until pumpkin is lightly caramelised and tender. Remove to a bowl to cool. Mash pumpkin with a fork or with a potato masher. Use to fill kutap, as directed.

SESAME SEED BREAD RINGS simit

Many versions of these sesame seed-encrusted bread rings can be found throughout the Eastern Mediterranean. Some are sweet and some are savoury. In Greece, slightly sweetened sesame *galettes* appear in pretzel-like plaited wreaths – these are known as *koulouria*. In Turkey, fat bagel-like rings are known as *simit*. Street vendors sell simit from mobile carts, or piled high on trays balanced on their heads. Other similar but different varieties are known as *ka'kat* in Israel and Egypt. In Lebanon, sesame bread is shaped into large flat discs with a hole at one end so that the bread can be threaded onto poles attached to handcarts. This Lebanese version is called *ka'aké*, but I affectionately call it 'handbag bread', because the loaves look for all the world like handbags, complete with carry handles.

1 cup lukewarm water

1 teaspoon active dry yeast

1 tablespoon sugar

2 cups bread flour,
plus extra for kneading and rolling

½ teaspoon salt

30g butter, melted

1 egg beaten with 1 tablespoon water,
for glazing

¼ cup sesame seeds

makes 12

1 Place ½ cup of the measured lukewarm water in a large bowl and sprinkle with yeast and sugar. Set aside for 5–10 minutes until the mixture foams, indicating that the yeast is activated. Stir in remaining water.

2 Gradually add 2 cups of measured flour, stirring to form a thick paste. Set aside to rest for 10 minutes.

3 Stir in salt and melted butter. Now, continue to add more flour, a little at a time while stirring with one hand until dough cannot take any more flour. Transfer to a lightly floured surface and knead for 10 minutes until smooth and elastic.

4 Lightly oil bowl and return dough to bowl. Cover with a damp tea towel or with plastic wrap and set aside to rise for 1 hour, or until doubled in volume.

5 Punch down dough with your fist and divide into 12 portions. On a lightly floured surface, roll each portion into a cigar-shaped rope 15cm long, then loop the ends together to form a circle. Place dough circles on lightly oiled baking sheets, allowing space for the bread to rise. Cover with a damp cloth or plastic wrap and set in a warm place to rise for 30 minutes, or until doubled in volume.

6 Preheat oven to 200°C. Brush bread rings with egg glaze and sprinkle with sesame seeds. Bake for 20–25 minutes, or until golden brown and bread rings sound hollow when tapped on the base.

pita pie filled with lamb & nutty rice ouzi

Ouzi is a typical pie-like, savoury pastry dish believed to have originated in the Syrian city of Damascus. However, we found this version in a great sidewalk café in the rebuilt centre of Beirut that is known as Downtown. Perhaps it should also be noted that in some Middle Eastern countries, ouzi refers to a whole baby lamb stuffed with rice.

For this particular pie-like ouzi, a mixture of lamb, nuts and rice is wrapped in a thin coating of pita bread dough and cooked until crisp. Once the shell is fractured, the perfume of the aromatic filling bursts into the air stimulating the appetite. A quick version can be made using store-bought puff pastry instead of pita bread dough.

142

1 tablespoon olive oil

150g lamb mince

1 tablespoon grated fresh ginger

3 cloves garlic, chopped

1 green chilli, seeds removed,
flesh chopped

1 teaspoon cardamom pods, crushed to open

1 teaspoon ground cinnamon

¼ teaspoon each ground cumin,
coriander, allspice, nutmeg

½ cup basmati rice

1 cup chicken stock

¼ cup toasted pistachio nuts

¼ cup toasted pine nuts

¼ cup toasted almonds

sea salt & freshly ground black pepper

½ recipe pita bread dough (see page 134)

yoghurt to serve

serves 4

1 Heat a frying pan, add oil and lamb mince to brown, separating mince as it cooks over a medium-high heat, stirring regularly. Add fresh ginger, garlic, chilli and dried spices and cook for 1 minute.

2 Stir in rice and chicken stock and bring to the boil, then turn down heat, cover pan and simmer gently for 5–8 minutes or until all liquid has been absorbed. Transfer mixture to a bowl. Stir in toasted nuts and season well with salt and pepper. Set aside to cool.

3 Preheat oven to 200°C. Divide pita bread dough into 4 portions. On a lightly floured surface, roll out each portion of dough as thinly as possible to form a large circle. Divide filling by 4 and place 1 portion in the centre of each circle of dough. Bundle up the edges of dough to cover filling and form 4 rounded parcels. Place parcels on a baking sheet with any seams hidden on the under-side – the parcels will look like smooth domes. Pierce a small incision in the centre of each dome to allow steam to escape during cooking.

4 Bake for 20–30 minutes or until the pita is puffed and golden brown. Serve hot with yoghurt on the side, as a sauce.

PARCHMENT BREAD lavoush

Serve parchment bread with any Middle Eastern dip, in the mezze tradition, along with a bowl of briny black olives and a posy of fresh mint leaves.

2¼ cups flour, plus extra for kneading & rolling
½ cup durum wheat semolina
1 teaspoon sea salt
1 teaspoon sugar
1 small egg, lightly beaten
200ml milk
¼ cup olive oil

makes 36

1 Combine flour, semolina, salt and sugar in a large bowl and make a well in the centre. Combine egg, milk and olive oil and pour into the well. Mix with a wooden spoon, then bring dough together with your hands.

2 Remove dough to a surface dusted with flour and lightly knead. Cover with plastic wrap and chill in the fridge for one hour.

3 Heat oven to 180°C. Line 2 baking trays with non-stick baking paper. Remove dough from fridge. On a lightly floured work surface, break off small portions of dough and roll out very thinly with a rolling pin.

4 Place rolled dough on prepared trays, prick entire surface of each sheet with a fork, then bake for 7–10 minutes until dry and pale golden brown. In some ovens you may need to turn the parchment sheets half way through cooking so that they brown evenly.

5 Parchment bread will stay crisp stored in an airtight container for up to a week. After 1 week the parchment sheets may need 3–5 minutes in a moderate oven to revive their crispness. Alternatively, dough can be frozen for up to 1 month, then defrosted for future use.

(see photograph, page 150)

ISTANBUL

The labyrinthine pathways of Istanbul's covered Grand Bazaar lie before us, enticingly. Known as the oldest and largest shopping mall in the world, this is a shopper's paradise. The seemingly endless array of goods for sale is certainly interesting, but it is the building that fascinates me most, along with the age-old rituals that continue within. A criss-cross of ancient vaulted ceilings and decorated archways cover the milieu of exotic smells, theatrical bartering, animated banter and tea drinking. At intersections there are water fountains, for refreshment and for cleansing before prayer, complete with ornate taps and metal cups suspended by chains.

Within the Grand Bazaar, the Turkish delight stalls are truly a delight. Soft rainbow colours cascade over bench-top displays where every shape, size, colour and flavour imaginable is neatly arranged in rows, according to type. Some are plain, some perfumed, and others are studded with nuts or dried fruits. There are also rolled versions of this translucent jellied sweet – spiral-centred logs thickly coated in desiccated coconut.

We meander down a lane leading out of the covered bazaar to an alternative shopping environment. The streets here are lined with general stores selling household items, hardware and so on, probably intended for a local clientele. But I find this a great place to increase my growing collection of authentic Middle Eastern food-styling props. I buy tiny tea glasses delicately edged in gold, a traditional brass Turkish coffee-pot, and some hand-hewn wooden spoons.

Crossing the suspension bridge that spans the Bosphorus takes us from Asia back to Europe, as Istanbul exists on both continents with this bridge connecting the two. Long slender fishing rods dangle from the bridge in a continuous row, bobbing up and down like streamers strewn over the side.

We're on our way to a place called Ortaköy, which was once a small fishing village, and is just a short trip up the coast. Here beside the Bosphorus in a carnival-like scene is an open-air market, with stalls selling crafts, linen and suchlike. A man is selling colourful balloons from a large bunch, and people we pass are eating candied sweets that look like multi-coloured sticky toffee wound around a stick. There are all sorts of food stalls too, selling, rather unexpectedly, stuffed potatoes, sandwiches, and a type of crêpe.

My first impressions are of a mouth-watering scent. There's smoke emanating from a charcoal grill so we head in that direction to investigate. Long sausage-shaped meats are turning slowly on small spits suspended over the grill. Fat languorously drips onto the charcoal and causes it to smoulder. The chef in attendance tells us these are *kokoreç* and offers us a slice that he cuts from a cooked section. With the hot juices running down our chins, we discover we are eating grilled and seasoned mutton intestines, which taste meaty, earthy and extremely rich. The friendly vendor does not seem too disappointed when we don't buy a portion or two to take away with us. Instead, we stop at a café for Turkish coffee and a refreshing yoghurt drink and sit for a while enjoying the relaxed weekend scene.

All too soon another day is over and we need to find a taxi to take us back into town. We begin walking along the main road, past grand palaces and tea gardens and soon we come to the central kiosk of a taxi company. Here we meet the most charming gentleman, who just happens to be the owner of the taxi company. We enjoy taking tea and chatting to him while we wait for a taxi. In the end our new friend offers to drive us himself and we are kindly delivered into town with much goodwill and sparkling conversation.

We have hurried back into Istanbul because tonight we have a date with some Whirling Dervishes. Earlier I had come across a flyer advertising a cultural performance by musicians and Whirling Dervishes, a mystic ritual I have long found fascinating and been eager to witness.

The flyer explains that a group of Whirling Dervishes perform every Saturday evening in the exhibition hall, platform number one at Istanbul's Sirkeci Central Train Station. This remarkable building was the destination of the famed rail experience known as the Orient Express. Posters of the carriages line the walls of a tea-room where we stop for refreshments while waiting for the performance to commence.

The Whirling Dervishes trace their origin to the thirteenth-century Ottoman Empire. The Dervishes, also known as the

Mevlana Order, are Sufis, a spiritual offshoot of Islam. There is a link here, as the founder of the Sufi mystic order blended food and spirituality in his teachings, likening cooking to the development of spiritual knowledge. The most highly regarded chef in Turkish history, Ateflbaz Veli, was also a thirteenth-century Dervish.

Ushered into the exhibition hall, we sit quietly in dim light taking in the faded beauty of the room where the only remnants of grandeur are well-worn tiles, dusty archways and fluted pillars, and coloured-glass windows.

Strange haunting music begins from a small band of traditional musicians. Music plays an integral part of the Whirling Dervishes search for spirituality. The Dervishes enter the room wearing tall hats and sweeping black cloaks. We watch in anticipation as the ritual dance ceremony, known as the Sema, begins.

The Sema consists of several structured stages with different meanings, so the whirling gently stops and starts throughout the performance. The turns become increasingly dynamic as the individual Dervishes strive to achieve a state compared to mystical flight or transcendental meditation. This ritual whirling is considered an act of love and faith. I have read that the *semazens,* the ones who whirl, do so to consciously participate in the shared revolution of all existence.

The cloaks are removed revealing long, wide, white or coloured skirts. The Dervishes extend their arms, the right palm faces up and the left palm faces down. And they begin to whirl. Silently spinning as if in a trance, their heads have fallen gently to one side, their eyes are closed and their faces are serenely blank. With their voluminous skirts twirling about them, they look like graceful human spinning tops.

We sit among the silent audience, transfixed by this sight of spinning and flowing human movement. The Dervishes seem to whirl fluidly for what seems like ten or twenty minutes at most. In fact, we watch this ceremony for a full hour. This seven centuries-old ritual is believed to enrich not only the Dervishes but also the Earth and the wellbeing of humanity as a whole. And at the end I too am left with a deep feeling of tranquillity.

&pickled preserved

pickled vegetables, vine leaves, jam, spoon sweets

BLACK LEMO

ED LEMON WHOLE

Pickled and preserved foods play a big part in the diet of Middle Eastern peoples. For countless generations Middle Eastern cooks have preserved all manner of vegetables, leaves, fruits, peel and flowers in the important process of putting away seasonal foods for later. This process can be likened to bottling sunlight, storing it up to brighten the long dark days of winter.

Known as *torshis* in Persian, pickles often accompany various rice dishes, kebabs and fried meats, or may be served as part of a first-course mezze selection. It is generally believed that pickles stimulate the appetite and are good for the health, as the acidity aids digestion. Vegetables and fruits are pickled in strong cider or grape vinegar with a variety of spices such as chilli, cardamom, turmeric and ginger, as well as many different seeds such as fennel, anise, coriander, poppy and mustard seeds. Some people even drink the sour preserving liquid, which is thirst-quenching in the heat of the day.

Every home has a private store of pickles. Harvested in season and when plentiful, fragrant and full of flavour, a reserve of fruits and vegetables is preserved and stored for use throughout the year. Pickles are very popular, so if home supplies are depleted, these can be supplemented with store-bought versions, as throughout the Middle East there are whole shops dedicated to pickled foods.

Some unusual preserves are unique to the Middle East, like tiny nut-stuffed eggplants pickled in vinegar and salt with spices, and sometimes tied into parcels with string or wrapped in vine leaves. Watermelon flesh is made into jam, and even the rind of watermelon is made into a curious pickle. We relish savoury pickled grapes in Turkey. We taste pickled tomatoes in Turkey and Azerbaijan, and find homemade jars of these for sale in the vast and astonishing local food market.

Fruits of the region were first preserved in honey and later in sugar. Many fruits, such as melons, apricots, cherries, plums, quinces, grapes and figs, are preserved whole and candied in thick syrup. Oranges are preserved in various jams and the peel is crystallised or candied. Sweet, juicy carrots are made into jam during the winter months when fruits are not available. Many jams are accented with cardamom seeds, a favourite flavouring for all preserves of Persian origin.

From ancient times, many dishes of sweets and preserves have been made from perfumed flower petals. Drying preserves the petals, and scented floral waters, such as rose water and orange flower water, are produced by distillation.

When we meet with our Azerbaijani friend, Zaur Aliyev, at his home in a suburb of Baku, we are offered tea. This comes in small glasses set on a tray, along with spoon sweets – rose petal jam and very sticky whole fruit conserves of fig and melon. Like jam, but so syrupy-thick that the fruit is almost candied, spoon sweets are eaten by the teaspoonful, providing a sugar boost at any time of day. Zaur tells us that spoon sweets are sometimes stirred into tea to add body and sweetness. We do this, and the tea is delicious.

Drying and salting are two other preserving processes utilised by Middle Eastern cooks. Whole limes are salted and dried, resulting in darkened, shrivelled, desiccated fruit that lasts indefinitely. To do this, fresh limes are boiled in highly salted water for a few minutes, then left to dry in the sun. When dry, these limes are used to add an unusual aromatic and tangy-sour flavour to various soups and stews.

Middle Eastern people have always had a great love of sour flavours. Pickles are made with vinegar and salt and are always sour, never sweetened. Verjuice, made from the sour juice of unripe green grapes, is popularly used to add sharpness to many dishes of Persian origin. Vine leaves are also pickled in a process that has not changed since early times.

There are two ways of preserving vine leaves: in dry salt or in a wet, salty mixture called brine. The best method is to tightly pack liberally salted layers of vine leaves into sterilised airtight jars and seal well. Or layer leaves in a jar, then cover with heavily salted water. Either way, choose similar-sized tender leaves that are not too young and fragile nor too old and hard, and wash and dry the leaves well before preserving.

PICKLED STUFFED BABY EGGPLANT

We regularly came across these pickled stuffed baby eggplants, especially in specialised preserve stores that are the equivalent of delicatessens. Tiny eggplants are perfect to stuff and serve whole as mezze. Preserving these stuffed eggplants in vinegar is a unique practice that I have not seen outside the Middle East.

12 very small round eggplants

stuffing
5 cloves garlic, chopped
1 teaspoon sea salt
¼ cup finely chopped fresh parsley
¼ cup walnuts, coarsely chopped

pickling liquid
2 cups white wine vinegar
1 cup water
3 dried red chillies

makes 12

1 Cut a slit in the middle of each eggplant. Bring a saucepan of water to the boil, add eggplants to the saucepan and simmer for 10 minutes until tender — keep a plate on top of eggplants so they are fully submerged during cooking. Drain and set aside on paper towels to cool a little.

2 Combine stuffing ingredients and spoon a little into the cavity of each eggplant. Tightly pack eggplants into a large sterilised jar. Turn jar upside-down over a bowl to drain overnight.

3 Next day, combine vinegar, water and chillies and pour over eggplants to cover completely. Seal jar and leave to sit in a cool place for 2–3 weeks before eating. Refrigerate after opening.

4 For a less acidic-tasting pickle, cover eggplants with olive oil instead of pickling liquid and store in the same manner.

151

pickled mixed vegetables

Middle Eastern pickles are preserved in vinegar, not brine, and are always sour. So, while sugar is not traditionally added, I like to add a little to take the bite off these pickles. You can leave out the sugar if you prefer and you can use a different selection of vegetables depending on what is in season. Often in the Middle East I found that beetroot was added to the mix so that the other vegetables take on a distinctive bright pink hue. Pickled vegetables seemed to appear on the table as part of the mezze before nearly every meal.

2 cups white wine vinegar

¼ cup water

3 tablespoons sugar

1 tablespoon coriander seeds

½ teaspoon whole peppercorns

2 tablespoons salt

1 cup cauliflower florets

2 large carrots, peeled & cut into sticks or 250g baby carrots, peeled

1 yellow pepper, seeds removed, flesh sliced

1 red pepper, seeds removed, flesh sliced

2 fennel bulbs, trimmed & sliced

6 cloves garlic, peeled

¼ cup chopped fresh parsley

serves 8–10

1 Place vinegar, water, sugar, spices and salt in a preserving pan or large saucepan. Bring to the boil, stirring until sugar dissolves.

2 Add prepared vegetables and bring mixture back to the boil, then simmer for 2 minutes.

3 Remove vegetables and pack into a sterilised jar. Pour over pickling liquid and seal jar securely. Store for 1 month before using. Once opened, store in the refrigerator. Serve as a mezze or side dish.

(see photograph, page 150)

STUFFED VINE LEAVES dolmah

Stuffed vine leaves are prevalent throughout the Middle East where they are invariably called dolmah. Their popularity even spread to the Balkans with the Ottoman Empire. They may be served hot or cold, and may be stuffed with rice or meat. For a meat-stuffing recipe, use the one for stuffed vegetables (see page 93).

You can use fresh or brined vine leaves to encase the filling. If using fresh leaves, select medium-coloured leaves that are not too young. In Iraq, spinach leaves are often used as the wrapping ingredient, with blanched cabbage leaves also used in place of vine leaves.

225g fresh medium-coloured vine leaves
(or see how to preserve vine leaves, page 149)

2 tablespoons lemon juice

2 tablespoons olive oil

stuffing mix

2 onions, finely chopped

2 tablespoons olive oil

I cup basmati rice

2 cups water

2 tablespoons currants

2 tablespoons pine nuts

2 tablespoons chopped fresh parsley

sea salt & freshly ground black pepper

½ teaspoon ground allspice

½ teaspoon ground cinnamon

serves 6

1 Place vine leaves in a bowl, cover with boiling water and leave to soak for 5 minutes, then rinse well. Remove stalks from vine leaves.

2 Meanwhile, make the stuffing. Heat a saucepan, add oil and onions and cook over a medium heat until softened but not coloured. Add rice and stir to coat with oil, then add remaining ingredients and cook gently for 15 minutes, stirring regularly until rice is tender to the bite. Set aside to cool.

3 Place I tablespoonful of filling in the centre of each vine leaf, fold edges over and roll up. Repeat with all vine leaves, then pack formed parcels tightly into a saucepan. Pour in enough boiling water to just cover parcels. Drizzle with olive oil and lemon juice.

4 Cover pan with lid and simmer vine leaves over a medium heat for 30 minutes or until tender. Transfer stuffed vine leaves to a serving platter and set aside to cool. Serve at room temperature.

(see photograph, page 156)

pickled tomatoes

Tomatoes are one of the more unusual vegetables pickled by Middle Eastern cooks. This particular sour pickle is popular in Eastern Mediterranean countries, such as Turkey, where the glut of summer tomatoes tends to be preserved to brighten up winter months.

500g small firm tomatoes, washed
I tablespoon sea salt
I teaspoon ground black pepper
I teaspoon each paprika & dried coriander
I teaspoon dried mint
4 cloves garlic, sliced
2 cups red wine vinegar

makes 3 x 300ml jars

1 With the tip of a sharp knife cut a cross in the tomatoes at the end from where the stems have been removed. Sprinkle salt into each cross and turn tomatoes upside-down to drain on paper towels for 2–3 hours.

2 Combine pepper, paprika, coriander and dried mint and sprinkle a little into the cross in each tomato. Pack tomatoes into wide-mouthed sterilised jars interspersed with slices of garlic.

3 Pour vinegar into jars to completely cover tomatoes. Seal jars and shake gently to release any pockets of air. Store in a cool dark place for 2 weeks before using as part of mezze or as an accompaniment to fish, chicken or meat dishes.

TURKISH PICKLED GRAPES

Grapes are eaten fresh, and dried, of course, as raisins and sultanas, but grapes can also be preserved, creating these refreshing titbits and showing just how resourceful Middle Eastern cooks are.

1kg small seedless green or red grapes
1 tablespoon mustard seeds
1½ cups white wine vinegar

makes 2 x 300ml jars

1 Separate bunches of grapes into clusters of 2–3 grapes. Pack half the grapes into sterilised wide-mouthed jars.

2 Crush remaining grapes, strain juice and discard pulp. Measure the juice. Place grape juice and an equal quantity of white wine vinegar in a saucepan. Add mustard seeds and bring to the boil, then pour the hot liquid over grapes.

3 Seal jars and store in a cool dark place for 1 month before using.

WATERMELON JAM

Watermelon and even watermelon rind are two of the more unusual jam ingredients typical of the Middle Eastern kitchen. Less like a jam and more like a conserve, this method of layering fruit with sugar, then leaving it to stand, encourages the pieces of fruit to hold together and turn into glossy, almost candied, nuggets suspended in a sugar syrup.

1.5kg watermelon
3 cups sugar
juice of 2 lemons

makes 4 x 300ml jars

1 Remove rind from watermelon. Dice watermelon flesh, removing any seeds. Place a layer of diced watermelon in a bowl, sprinkle with a layer of sugar. Continue to layer until all watermelon and sugar have been used. Cover bowl and stand in a cool place for 4 hours.

2 Transfer mixture to a preserving pan. Add lemon juice and cook over moderate heat for 45–50 minutes, stirring frequently, until mixture is thick.

3 Skim off any foam with a metal spoon. Ladle watermelon jam into hot, sterilised jars and seal immediately.

CANDIED ORANGE PEEL

Glistening with sweetness, candied orange peel is commonly eaten as a tasty sweet-meat or as a spoon sweet to be enjoyed alongside a glass of hot tea.

5 oranges
3 cups sugar
3 cups water
I tablespoon orange flower water

makes 3 x 300ml jars

1 Remove rind from oranges in thick strips. Scrape off any white pith and reserve orange flesh for fruit salad, if desired. Place strips of rind in a bowl, cover with cold water and leave to soak overnight.

2 The following day, transfer rind to a saucepan and discard soaking liquid. Cover rind with fresh cold water and bring to the boil, then simmer for 30 minutes, adding extra water if necessary. Drain and discard cooking liquid.

3 Combine sugar and measured water in the saucepan and bring to the boil, stirring until sugar dissolves. Add rind and simmer for 30 minutes. Lastly stir in orange flower water.

4 Fill sterilised jars with candied peel and syrup. Store in a cool dark place for 2 weeks before eating.

CARROT JAM

In Middle Eastern countries, jams are eaten in completely different ways to in the West. Jams like this one will be served with tea, never on toast, but eaten simply from a spoon as an extra sweetener for the tea. And some fairly unique fruits and also vegetables are typically used to make these jams, for example, eggplant, walnuts, grapes, rose petals, pumpkin, tomatoes and, of course, carrots.

250g (2 large) carrots, peeled & grated
I¼ cups sugar
finely grated zest of 2 lemons
4 cardamom pods, split

makes 2 x 300ml jars

1 Place all ingredients in a saucepan and heat gently, stirring until sugar dissolves. Raise the heat and boil for 10 minutes until mixture is thick and syrupy.

2 Pour jam into warm sterilised jars and seal well. Carrot jam can be eaten immediately or will last well stored in a cool dark place for up to a year.

floral confections
syrups, sweet-meats, pastries, puddings

Floral confections, hauntingly perfumed syrup-drenched pastries, and other sweets whose origins are shared can be found all over the Middle East. Pastry shops abound, though here these are known as sweet shops. And the sweet treats of preference seem to be fragrant creations.

People of these lands are very fond of perfumed foods. Voluptuously scented floral waters are included in pastries, and scented sugar syrup is used to drench others. Rose is the preferred flavouring for *lokum* (Turkish delight), and rose petal jam is eaten as a spoon sweet. Dried petals or tiny dried rosebuds are used for making a sweet tea infusion and for this purpose pretty little rosebuds can be purchased from spice souks, where they are sold loose from huge sacks.

For many centuries, the concentrated aromatic essence of rose and orange blossoms has been extracted from harvested petals by distillation. Floral waters are used as personal scent or to perfume an entire room. We were often offered floral waters to sprinkle and cleanse our hands before or after a meal, or between courses. These floral preparations are also used as ingredients in many different sweets, puddings and pastries. I've even tasted stews, coffee and *tisanes* that contain rose or orange flower water.

The best floral waters I've tasted are homemade. In a cool, dark room on a copper still heated over a charcoal brazier, steam moves through the petals, condenses and cools, and perfumed water falls drop by drop into a waiting bottle, ready for use in cooking or as a toilet water. The name of the special variety of rose used for distillation is Damask, and the pure scent is extracted and exported to many parts of the world.

In Bahrain, I discover bottles and bottles of floral waters made from the most startling blooms. There's rose and orange blossom, of course, but also quince flower, pussy willow, palm flower and many more. Anise seeds and fennel seeds are also distilled for use in cooking.

One day while stuck in chaotic traffic on the outskirts of Beirut, Lebanon, a brightly lit sweet shop attracts my eye. I need to investigate the hypnotic display of sweets, shining like brilliant jewels under the bright lighting.

I gaze in amazement at complex arrangements of sticky macaroons and piles of perfect pastries, some saturated in thick rivulets of perfumed syrups, some encasing fillings of dried fruits or nuts or cream. Another countertop is covered with huge slabs of halva and other coconut ice-like slabs of sweetness available in different colours and flavours, some spread with chocolate.

There are an outrageous number of daintily moulded biscuits, slices, honey-drenched pastries, and all the famous sweets of Lebanon. Every diminutive item is exquisitely formed and completely ambrosial. Imagine miniature bird's nests of shredded pastry with pistachio nuts placed like eggs in the nest. Or paper cases holding intricately formed gossamer turbans of sesame candy floss.

The pastry chef in me is full of technical praise; the child in me feels like this is the first time I have ever set foot in a candy store. The smiling assistants offer me a taste of the rose coconut-ice creation by slicing off a slither. My murmurs of appreciation prompt more offerings – taste after taste almost to the point of embarrassment. I get the impression that if I wanted to stay and try every single item they would let me.

These delicious sweets are either sold by the kilo or by the dozen, so it's possible to choose a variety of types. In an attempt to tear myself away I purchase an assortment for indulging in later. Sweet pastries such as these are generally reserved to enjoy with tea or coffee, to honour guests, or to give as a gift. It is very much part of the traditional practice of hospitality to arrive at someone's home with some offering, usually food. Although sweets are adored with a passion, they are not traditionally eaten for dessert. Puddings are most likely to be reserved for celebrations or bereavements when the sweetness is thought to lift the spirits during sadness.

FLORAL SUGAR SYRUP qatr

This is the base syrup used to drench many different Middle Eastern pastries, such as baklava, *basbousa* and *remaush el set*. In its simplest form, this syrup can be drizzled over fruit salad to infuse the fruit with its sweet floral flavour.

2 cups sugar
¾ cup water
juice of 2 lemons
1–2 teaspoons rose water or
orange flower water, to taste

makes 2 cups

1 Combine all ingredients, except floral water, in a saucepan. Bring to the boil, stirring until sugar dissolves.

2 Simmer gently for 5 minutes to form a syrup. Stir in chosen floral water to taste.

3 Set aside to cool, then use as particular recipe directs. Can be stored indefinitely in the refrigerator.

REMAUSH EL SET

Ibrahim Rashed, the very talented Egyptian chef on the *Sun Boat IV* not only showed me how to make these divine biscuits but kindly wrote out the recipe for me as well.

175g butter, softened
½ cup icing sugar
1 egg
½ teaspoon vanilla extract
⅓ cup fine desiccated coconut
1¼ cups plus 1 tablespoon flour
26 almonds
1x floral sugar syrup recipe (see above)

makes 26

1 Preheat oven to 175°C. Line two baking trays with non-stick baking paper.

2 Combine butter and icing sugar in a bowl and beat until creamy. Beat in egg and vanilla. Then add coconut and flour and beat briefly, just enough to form a firm dough.

3 Mould tablespoonfuls of dough into teardrop-shaped biscuits and place on the prepared baking trays. Press an almond on top of each biscuit.

4 Bake for 15 minutes or until pale golden and firm. Remove to a deep-sided dish and pour over cold sugar syrup while the biscuits are still hot.

BAKLAVA

Often associated with celebrations, multi-layered *baklava* is one of the most magnificent of all Middle Eastern syrup-drenched pastries. While several Middle Eastern countries may claim to be the original home of baklava, it is generally believed to be an Ottoman legacy. Walnuts are most commonly used to fill baklava, although almonds work just as well, as do pistachio nuts, which are considered the most highly prized.

3 cups (400g) walnuts,
blanched almonds or pistachio nuts

½ cup caster sugar

I teaspoon ground cinnamon
or cardamom

6 sheets filo pastry

200g clarified butter, melted

2 x floral sugar syrup recipe (see page 162)

makes 24

1 Combine chosen nuts, sugar and cinnamon or cardamom in the bowl of a food processor and process just until nuts are finely chopped, then set aside.

2 Preheat oven to 180°C. Grease a 22cm x 30cm baking pan with some of the melted butter. Remove filo sheets from packet and lay on a work surface covered with a damp cloth to prevent them from drying out.

3 Fold 1 filo sheet in half and lay in the bottom of the pan, then brush with some melted butter. Place another folded filo sheet on top and brush with butter. Repeat this process one more time with another filo sheet to give 6 layers of filo.

4 Spread ground nut mixture over filo layers in the pan. Lay another folded filo sheet on top of nuts, then brush with butter. Continue this process until all filo has been used. Brush top layer of filo with remaining melted butter.

5 Carefully cut through layers to make 3cm diamonds or squares. Bake for 45–50 minutes or until golden brown. Remove pan from oven and pour over cold floral sugar syrup to saturate baklava. Cut again, then remove from pan. Store in an airtight container and serve at room temperature.

SEMOLINA HALVA SYRUP CAKE basbousa

Not to be confused with the huge slabs of sesame halva, made from sesame seed paste and sugar or honey that can be bought in souks – this syrup-drenched halva cake is just one example of the many different forms that halva takes.

125g butter, softened
¾ cup caster sugar
2 eggs
1½ cups fine semolina
1½ teaspoons baking powder
¾ cup plain yoghurt
18 whole blanched almonds to decorate
1x floral sugar syrup recipe (see page 162)

makes 18

1 Preheat oven to 180°C. Grease a 17cm x 27cm slice tin or line with non-stick baking paper, leaving an overhang on all sides.

2 In a bowl, beat butter and sugar until creamy. Beat in eggs one at a time. Sift semolina and baking powder and fold into butter mixture alternately with yoghurt.

3 Spread into prepared tin. Arrange almonds on top in rows so each slice will hold an almond when cake is cut. Bake for 30–35 minutes or until surface springs bake when pressed. Remove from oven. Pour cold syrup over hot cake while still in the tin.

4 Cut into diamonds or squares once completely cold. Stored in an airtight container, this syrup cake will last well for up to 5 days.

ROSE PETAL JAM

Eating rose petal jam is like immersing all your senses in an old-fashioned scented rose garden. This compelling floral nectar with supposed secret powers appears in the stories of the Arabian Nights.

50g perfumed dark red or pink rose petals

1 cup sugar

2 tablespoons pectin

juice of 1 lemon

1 cup water

1 teaspoon rose water (optional)

makes 2 cups

1 Roughly chop rose petals and place in a bowl with sugar. Cover and leave for 24 hours.

2 Next day, place rose petals and sugar, pectin, lemon juice and water in a preserving pan or large heavy-based saucepan. Bring to the boil, stirring until sugar dissolves, then simmer for 20 minutes.

3 Boil for 5 minutes until setting point is reached. Add rose water to increase flavour, if desired. Ladle into warm sterilised jars and seal well.

(see photograph, page 160)

167

ROSE WATER MERINGUES

These are not truly Middle Eastern, but are my contrivance. Rose water meringues mix remnants of French influence – left over from the days when Lebanon was a French protectorate – with rose water, a classic Middle Eastern flavouring.

Fragrant roses bloom in Syria, Lebanon and Turkey. The annual harvest of rose petals is used for the distillation of rose water, which in turn is used in many confections and also in some savoury dishes.

3 egg whites

1 cup caster sugar

1–2 teaspoons rose water

fresh rose petals & pomegranate seeds to serve

makes 20

1 Preheat oven to 100°C. Line 2 oven trays with non-stick baking paper.

2 Whisk egg whites until stiff but not dry. Add 1 tablespoonful of measured sugar and whisk until incorporated. Whisk in remaining sugar until mixture is glossy. Whisk in rose water.

3 Spoon small mounds of meringue onto prepared oven trays. Bake for 1 hour or until meringues are dry and crisp. Serve with pomegranate seeds and fresh rose petals, which are quite edible.

ROSE-SCENTED TURKISH DELIGHT *lokum*

Like many specialised confections, I find it takes a few tries to get a feel for the Turkish delight-making process and to understand the finished texture that you're aiming for. But once you've mastered the art this is a truly wonderful thing to be able to make and give to friends or loved ones.

2½ cups cold water

80g gelatine powder

3½ cups sugar

¼ teaspoon cream of tartar (tartaric acid)

I tablespoon lemon juice

I teaspoon rose water

½ teaspoon red food colouring

I cup icing sugar (confectioner's sugar)

makes 100

1 Lightly oil a 20cm square cake tin. Place water in a heavy-based saucepan. Sprinkle gelatine powder over water and leave for 5 minutes for gelatine to absorb water like a sponge.

2 Place saucepan over a gentle heat until gelatine dissolves. Stir in sugar, cream of tartar and lemon juice. Bring mixture to the boil, stirring continuously until sugar has dissolved. Continue to boil gently over a medium heat for 15 minutes. You will notice that the boiling bubbles will be small at first but become bigger when the mixture has thickened and is ready.

3 Remove saucepan from heat and stir in rose water to flavour and red food colouring so that the mixture turns bright pink. Pour mixture into prepared tin. Stand uncovered overnight to set.

4 Sift icing sugar onto a large cutting board, then turn out slab of Turkish delight onto the board. Cut into 2cm squares with a lightly oiled knife and toss squares to coat in icing sugar. Store Turkish delight in an airtight container with sheets of waxed paper separating each layer. Dust with extra icing sugar before serving.

tinkling
glasses
hot & cold beverages

A man rushes through the crowded street with a tray of small glasses filled with steaming amber-coloured tea. As he passes I can hear the glasses tinkling on the beaten copper tray. This scene is played out all over the Middle East every day, as tea is delivered from teahouses to waiting shopkeepers.

Amman, the capital city of Jordan, lies on a high plateau etched with maze-like streets that wind around seven hills and through often ramshackle buildings. There are newer parts of town too, but we prefer to explore the old medina.

Today we're enjoying window-shopping as I try and find a souk to investigate the local produce. I also want to buy a selection of classic little tea glasses. We stop at a type of general store that has a display of tea paraphernalia outside. The owner, Rani, invites us to take tea and pass the time of day. From then on, every time we walk past his shop, even several days later, Rani calls us in to share more tea and conversation. It seems remarkable to visit a large city and make a new friend so quickly.

A huge selection of drinks is available on the street, either from corner stalls or roaming vendors. Freshly squeezed fruit juice utilises every type of citrus fruit. There's mandarin, orange and blood orange when in season, and citron presse or Middle Eastern lemonade, made from fresh lemon juice and sugar. Other juices I find especially appealing are pomegranate juice, which sometimes has a little orange flower water added, and pretty pink watermelon juice – both are brilliant thirst-quenchers that work towards countering the heat of the day.

Tea is often favoured over coffee, as it is less expensive and is characteristically served in small tulip-shaped glasses. In Iran and Azerbaijan, tea is frequently served from an elaborate metal urn called a *samovar*. Apple tea is everywhere in Turkey – it tastes tangy yet sweet and can be bought in powdered form.

Other tea infusion ingredients can be purchased from the bazaars, where tangles of dried flowers and leaves are displayed in large sacks. Chamomile is common, as are mint, thyme, and rose. Hibiscus flower infusion is the tisane of choice in Egypt and iced tea made from these dried petals is also common. A type of tea can also be made from an infusion of pomegranate molasses or tamarind – both sour concoctions come highly sweetened with sugar. And rose or orange flower water added to boiling water makes an authentic and refreshing hot drink.

In Istanbul we drink *salep*, a powdered extract from a type of dried orchid tuber. When mixed with hot milk salep thickens to form a dense drink. Also in Turkey we taste *ayran*, a refreshing watered-down yoghurt drink, with salt added to taste. Various other Middle Eastern countries have a tradition of yoghurt drinks; each similar in composition but different in name.

Drinking coffee is a tradition that remains strong throughout the Middle East. The sweetness of the coffee is changeable according to the taste of the guests and to the occasion. For instance, though this custom is not always strictly applied, coffee is served bitter for funeral condolences.

Known variously as Arabic, Turkish or Lebanese coffee, little cups of thick coffee are readily available throughout these lands. Brewed in a small, brass coffee-pot with a wide base and long handle, so common in the Middle East, this coffee is served strong, black and sweet. Curiously, instant coffee is now common too and is often written up on menus as Nescafé.

Middle Eastern hospitality is legendary and is most frequently expressed to strangers through the offering of tea, coffee or food. According to the rules of Middle Eastern tradition, a host is honour bound to offer a least one cup of tea or coffee to welcome a guest. Whether in a tea house, a private home, or a shop, visitors are expected to accept this offering of conviviality and goodwill.

Whenever I am offered the chance to share refreshment and hospitality in this way I enjoy the experience immensely. Each sip of tea seems to taste of mystery, tradition and history, blended with human kindness and a warmth of hospitality that is unmatched. Taking tea in the medina is a truly priceless experience.

HIBISCUS JUICE

Hibiscus juice is actually an iced tea made from an infusion of dried hibiscus flowers, which are sold from piled-high baskets in the souks of Egypt. Each day when we returned to the lovely *Sun Boat IV* after a Nile-side excursion to one of the many ancient sites and monuments, we would be offered a cooling glass of chilled 'hibiscus juice'. This restorative ritual not only quenched our thirst but also calmed our spirits after dealing with the great hoards of tourists encountered along the way.

½ cup dried hibiscus flowers (or substitute hibiscus flower tea available from health food shops)

½–1 cup sugar

4 cups boiling water

serves 8

1 Place hibiscus flowers or tea in a teapot or jug. Pour on boiling water, stir, adding sugar to sweeten to taste. Leave to infuse for 5 minutes, then strain and drink as a hot tea infusion.

2 Or, for iced tea, leave the infusion to cool. Strain mixture and discard hibiscus flowers. Chill well before serving in small tea glasses.

MIDDLE EASTERN LEMONADE

Very sweet and almost syrupy, Middle Eastern lemonade is served in delicate little glasses. Sipped during the heat of the day, this is a most satisfying refreshment.

10 lemons

1 cup cold water

½–1 cup sugar, to taste

1–2 teaspoons orange flower water, or to taste

serves 6–8

1 Squeeze juice from lemons and place in a tall jug. Add water and sweeten to taste with sugar, stirring until sugar dissolves.

2 Stir in orange flower water, adding more to taste, if preferred. Chill well before serving in small decorative glasses.

ARABIC COFFEE

The fusion of cardamom and saffron with thick dark coffee makes a curious and delicious combination. Tiny thimbles of this coffee are often served with fresh dates, the sticky sweetness of which delightfully complements the bitterness of the coffee.

3 cups water

3 tablespoons ground coffee

I teaspoon cardamom seeds (coarsely ground)

½ teaspoon saffron threads

serves 6

1 Place water, coffee and spices in an Arabic coffee pot or a small saucepan and bring to the boil over a medium heat.

2 Remove from the heat and set aside for a few minutes to allow the coffee to settle and spices to infuse. This infused coffee should not need straining as the sediment settles at the bottom of the pot, leaving the coffee to be poured off the top.

3 Serve in very small cups or glasses.

YOGHURT DRINK ayran

Preparation of this healthy yoghurt drink is simplicity itself. Known in Turkey as *ayran,* the Arabs call it *laban shrab,* the Persians *abdug.* Versions known as *lassi* can even be found in India, and show how far this concept has spread. In Middle Eastern countries this traditional drink is served with quite a high proportion of added salt – consuming this salty liquid seems to have a cooling effect on the body – however, a light salting seems better suited to Western tastes.

I cup thick-style natural yoghurt

¼ cup iced water

pinch salt, or more to taste

serves 1

1 Blend together yoghurt, water and salt to taste. Chill well and serve.

176

AFTERWORD

'The traveller sees what he sees, the tourist sees what he has come to see.'
G K Chesterton

I surreptitiously negotiated the unlocking of a door that led to the roof of the ancient mosque. From the roof, the twin minarets in front of me looked impossibly tall. At the base of one minaret a door was ajar revealing the sight of its twin, framed in an ornate opening against a clear blue sky. Perfection.

I have been captured by the lure of the Middle East, each visit bringing new and immeasurable rewards. From the frantic commercial congestion of Cairo to majestic ruins and enigmatic desert scapes, the Middle East is full of endless variation. I am never disappointed.

Often referred to as 'the cradle of civilisation' this region has spawned three of the world's great religions: Islam, Judaism and Christianity. It is also the home to two of the great 'mother' civilisations of the world, Mesopotamia and the Nile Valley.

The era of the Pharaohs was layered with glorious art, architecture and embellishments; the Phoenicians established great maritime economies which are now being replicated in the modern day by countries such as Dubai. The Byzantium and Ottoman empires ruled and established vast commercial worlds.

I have travelled all the lands once contained within the Persian Empire. The countries of the Middle East are dynamic and welcoming, each unique region ready to be savoured. But Iran was the greatest surprise. Here I experienced amazement and joy and a need to pause for thought. Full of history and immeasurable beauty, Iran leaves you with a feeling that you will never see all it has to offer.

Although oil had little significance until the twentieth century, not all Middle-Eastern countries are oil rich. Egypt, Turkey, Jordan, Israel and Lebanon lack the prosperity that oil brings but they are still very rich in civilisation and hospitality.

Empires and invaders, including Alexander the Great, have come and gone, leaving a perception of instability. Don't be afraid of travelling in the Middle East. Decorum in terms of dress and behaviour will be rewarded with delightful interaction with local people. If you are respectful and open-minded, your time here will be enriched. All but a few in this sprawling region live in observance of peace, harmony and tolerance.

John Bougen

GLOSSARY

Ahwa — Arabic name for coffee

Al-Khaneh — The Treasury building at Petra, Jordan

Ayran — refreshing yoghurt drink, thinned with water and sometimes accented with fresh mint

Barberries — dried sour crimson berries. Substitute for currants

Basmati rice — a variety of fragrant, long-grain white rice

Biryani — saffron-spiced rice dish of Indian origin but often made in the Gulf States. Usually contains meat or chicken, or more unusually fish

Burghul — par-boiled ground or cracked wheat used as a starchy ingredient in cooking. Also known as bulgur wheat — may be finely or coarsely ground

Chai — Arabic name for tea

Circassian — displaced peoples of the Caucasus Mountains who fled to the Ottoman Empire when their lands were conquered by the Russians

Corniche — waterfront promenade

Date syrup — also known as date molasses, made by soaking dates in hot water, then straining the thick syrupy pulp for use in cooking

Dervishes — also known as Mevlana order, these are Sufi mystics who whirl in a ritual spiritual dance

Dried lime — dried form of special type of lime unique to the Middle East. The dried fruit is dark brown or black and has a strong tangy aroma. It can be found in Middle Eastern stores under a variety of names, such as Basrah lemon or Oman lemon. If unavailable, the best substitute is the peel of a fresh lemon or lime

Dried sour cherries — pitted cherries that are dried like raisins. Available from speciality food stores. Substitute raisins or fresh cherries, if unavailable

Dukkah — Egyptian spice and nut mix used as a dip for bread

Eesh shamsi — this bread is typical of Upper Egypt and is known as sun bread because it is left to rise and cook in the sun

Eggah — one of the Arabic names for certain egg dishes, such as omelettes, which are also known as kuku

Fava — broad beans

Feta — fresh white cheese that is pressed and sliced and stored in salty brine

Filo — also spelt as phyllo — paper-thin pastry used to make sweet and savoury dishes, such as baklava

Frankincense — tree sap used as a spicy chewing gum or burnt as incense

Ful medames — cooked mixture of broad beans served on bread with oil and lemon juice

Ghee — Indian name for clarified butter. Known as semneh in Arabic

Halloumi — originating in Cyprus this is a stretched curd cheese stored in brine

Halva — there are many forms of halva, some are homemade, others commercially produced, but all contain ground seeds or nuts of some type, often drenched in sugar syrup. Sesame halva, which is made commercially of ground sesame seeds and either honey or sugar, can be purchased from speciality food stores and some supermarkets

Indigo — blue-coloured laundry agent

sold in spice markets, used to brighten white fabrics and clothing

Karkadeeh — sweetened hibiscus flower tea of Egypt, brewed from dried deep-red hibiscus flower petals, may be served hot or cold

Kebab — skewered pieces of meat, chicken or vegetables that are grilled

Kefta or kofta — meatballs or flavoured mincemeat mixture moulded onto skewers and grilled

Khoresh — Persian name for a stew-like sauce, usually served with rice

Khubz — Arabic name for bread

Kokoreç — Turkish speciality of seasoned grilled mutton intestines

Kuku — Arabic type of omelette

Labneh — strained yoghurt that forms a type of fresh cheese

Lebanese cucumber — smaller sweeter variety of cucumber

Lokum — Arabic name for Turkish delight

Mastic — aromatic tree gum, powdered and used as a spice in sweet dishes, pastries and ice-cream

Medina — Old City that once would have been completely enclosed within defensive walls (ramparts)

Mezze — appetisers or first-course dishes. Also describes a way of eating — a series of small dishes served as an introduction to a meal

Muezzin — Muslim call to prayer

Muhallabicileri — Turkish milk-bar-cum-teahouse-cum-pudding shop

Nabatean — an early Arab people who built the ancient city of Petra

182

Nargileh — another name for hubbly bubbly tobacco water pipes

Orange flower water — distilled essence of orange blossoms used in cooking. Available from specialised food stores and some supermarkets

Ottoman — relating to the Turkish people during the Ottoman Empire of the late thirteenth century

Pain au levain — French bread made with a natural yeast starter

Persian — relating to ancient Persia or modern Iran

Pide — variety of Turkish flatbread

Pilaf — rice dish cooked by the absorption method, may be plain or have seasonings, fruit or nuts added

Pita bread — typical Middle Eastern round- or oval-shaped flatbread that puffs up and is hollow when cooked

Pomegranate molasses — highly reduced juice of pomegranates that forms a thick bittersweet syrup used in sauces, dips and dressings. Available from specialised food stores and some supermarkets

Purslane — dark green, rounded leaf herb with a slightly nutty flavour, used as a salad leaf

Romaine lettuce — also known as cos lettuce

Rose water — distilled scented water of rose petals, used in cooking. Available from specialised food stores and some supermarkets

Saffron — (*zaafaran*) deep-orange, aromatic, dried stigmas gathered from a special type of purple crocus flower. Saffron is a very expensive spice and is therefore sold in small quantities. Saffron is used to colour and flavour foods such as rice

Saj — very thin type of flatbread cooked on a dome-shaped hot plate

Salap — a powdered extract from a type of dried orchid tuber mixed with hot milk, which thickens to form a dense and warming drink

Samovar — metal hot-water urn for making tea

Sema — ritual spinning dance of Whirling Dervishes

Semazen — the name for Dervishes who whirl

Semneh — Arabic name for clarified butter, used as a cooking fat

Shisha — name for tobacco water pipe. Also known as nargileh or hubbly bubbly water pipe because of the sound that it makes when smoked

Siq — chasm

Souk — a market or collection of stalls whether permanently established within the medina, open-air, or transient

Spoon sweet — jam-like sweet conserve served and eaten from spoons, often to accompany tea

Sufi — religious mystic order, an offshoot of Islam

Sumac — ground reddish-purple berry peculiar to the Middle East, sumac has a sharp lemony taste and is used as a spice or lemon substitute. Available from specialised food stores and some supermarkets. Substitute lemon juice or finely grated zest if unavailable

Tahini — a thick beige-coloured paste made from toasted ground sesame seeds. Tahini may separate with time but remains edible, simply stir before using. Tahini can be found in health-food stores, Middle Eastern stores and some supermarkets. Best stored in the fridge to prevent rancidity

Tamarind — a tangy tropical fruit, available in pulp or concentrate. The pulp needs to be soaked and strained before use — the concentrate is easier to use because it has already been treated in this manner

Tandoor — a special type of oven, cylindrical in shape and most typical of India. Used to cook flatbreads in some parts of the Middle East

Tisane — a hot tea infusion, may be made with leaves, flowers or spices

Torshi — Persian name for pickled vegetables

Tulum — goat's cheese matured in goat's skin

Verjuice — the juice of unripe grapes used in place of vinegar or wine in cooking

Wharka — thin Moroccan pastry

Za'atar — spice mix of dried thyme, sumac and sesame seeds, most commonly sprinkled over flatbread

A note on Arabic words and translation:

As Arabic is written in script, any translation into English will be phonetic. English spellings therefore vary, as words are heard and written in different ways by different people. Take for example the dish of baba ghanoush, which I have seen spelt in many ways from baba ganoushe and baba ghannoouge to baba ghannuj and baba ghanouj. No spelling is necessarily incorrect but for the purpose of consistency, I have noted only one spelling for each Arabic word in this book.

index

185

ACKNOWLEDGEMENTS

This book is dedicated to the exuberant profusion and rich diversity that is Middle Eastern cooking – and to the warm, generous, hospitable people we encountered throughout this region. Our thanks and appreciation go to the following people for their assistance:

We are deeply grateful to various chefs, home cooks, old friends, and new acquaintances met by chance, for sharing so generously with us. Your time, genuine recipes and knowledge have given this book a truly authentic flavour.

Special thanks go to Asma (Dubai) for eloquently explaining Dubai's culinary history and for sending gifts of food. Thanks to Ragat and family for embracing us, for a welcoming meal, and lively dancing. Thank you Zauer Aliyev, sister Chimna, and cousin-in-law Savinj, of Baku, Azerbaijan, for a day of cooking, your gifts of recipes, and other kindnesses we will always fondly remember.

Julie Le Clerc would like to thank her Lebanese friends Elaine and Richard Corban and daughter Leza, and Greg Malouf (of MoMo Restaurant, Melbourne), and Greg's aunt, Houda Bouri, for their warm generosity and unmatched Lebanese hospitality.

Thanks goes to *Cuisine* magazine, where some recipes and words of this culinary story first appeared, albeit in another form. Plus, grateful thanks go to Bernice, Helen, Jo, Anna, and The Cat and the Fiddle for kindly lending additional and treasured props for food photography.

John Bougen would especially like to acknowledge our guide, Azita Zahirian Moghaddam, from Tourist Agency Iran. a-zm1984@yahoo.com

Thank you Peter Fulton, General Manager, Grand Hyatt, Dubai, for your kind hospitality. And for not only enabling us to enjoy the luxury of Hyatt's Middle Eastern Hotels, but also for putting us in contact with some exceptional in-house chefs. www.hyatt.com

We are indebted to Abercrombie and Kent for assistance during our Nile cruise onboard *Sun Boat IV.* Special credit goes to the executive chef on *Sun Boat IV,* Ibrahim Rashed, for unstintingly sharing your recipes and for allowing us into your kitchen to observe the preparation of many fine dishes. www.abercrombiekent.com

Thank you James Irving, once again, for your extraordinary 24-hour on-call travel agency service. jirving@mtatravel.com.au

We also wish to acknowledge Gulf Air, and in particular the general manager in Australia, Crammer Ball, for helping us experience the joy of travelling throughout the Middle East with ultimate ease and comfort. www.gulfairco.com

Our warmest thanks go to our publisher Bernice Beachman, senior editor Philippa Gerrard and editor Louise Armstrong – our talented, wise and supportive team at Penguin Books (NZ). And our thanks and applause also goes to award-winning designer Athena Sommerfeld for weaving a mountain of information into this visual feast.

PENGUIN BOOKS
Published by the Penguin Group
Penguin Group (NZ),
67 Apollo Drive, Mairangi Bay,
Auckland 1310, New Zealand
(a division of Pearson New Zealand Ltd)
Penguin Group (USA) Inc., 375 Hudson Street,
New York, New York 10014, USA
Penguin Group (Canada),
90 Eglinton Avenue East, Suite 700, Toronto,
Ontario, M4P 2Y3, Canada
(a division of Pearson Penguin Canada Inc.)
Penguin Books Ltd,
80 Strand, London, WC2R 0RL, England
Penguin Ireland,
25 St Stephen's Green, Dublin 2, Ireland
(a division of Penguin Books Ltd)
Penguin Group (Australia),
250 Camberwell Road, Camberwell,
Victoria 3124, Australia
(a division of Pearson Australia Group Pty Ltd)
Penguin Books India Pvt Ltd,
11, Community Centre,
Panchsheel Park, New Delhi - 110 017, India
Penguin Books (South Africa) (Pty) Ltd,
24 Sturdee Avenue,
Rosebank, Johannesburg 2196, South Africa

Penguin Books Ltd, Registered Offices:
80 Strand, London, WC2R 0RL, England

First published by Penguin Group (NZ), 2006
1 3 5 7 9 10 8 6 4 2

Designed and typeset by Athena Sommerfeld
Prepress by Image Centre Ltd
Printed in China through Bookbuilders,
Hong Kong

ISBN – 13: 978 0 14 302033 2
ISBN – 10: 0 14 302033 1
A catalogue record for this book is available
from the National Library of New Zealand.

www.penguin.co.nz